TABLE OF CONTENTS

PREFACE

To stay fresh in the human resource (HR) management field, individuals must continually update their knowledge and skills. The 21st-century U.S. workplace will require HR professionals to respond to widely varying concerns: the changing nature of work, re-engineered workplaces, virtual offices, employee rights, worker literacy, demographic changes and global competition, for example.

As the profession changes, so does the body of knowledge that HR professionals must master. Fortunately, the HR Certification Institute has conducted extensive research to identify the PHR and SPHR Body of Knowledge. From this process, new and revised test specifications are developed and updated in all HR functional areas—specifications that form the blueprint for development of the HR Certification Institute certification exams.

The HR Certification Institute's mission is to develop and deliver the highest quality certification programs that validate mastery in the field of human resource management and contribute to the continued improvement of individual and organizational performance. Depending on experience and education levels, individuals can obtain certification as a Professional in Human Resources (PHR) or a Senior Professional in Human Resources (SPHR). This guide is an aid to candidates considering taking one of these exams. It is designed to help candidates understand the certification process and allow them to assess their level of preparedness.

ACKNOWLEDGMENTS

This publication would not have been possible without the contribution of the HR Certification Institute board of directors and the many volunteers who help in item and exam development. The work of these dedicated volunteers forms the basis for the content of this publication.

Volunteers are the heart and soul of our certification program. All volunteers are certified professionals who have successfully passed the exams. They write and review draft test items, establish passing or cut scores and support the Institute in its mission.

The HR Certification Institute gratefully recognizes the special contributions made over many years by Raymond B. Weinberg, SPHR, CCP, the original author of this certification guide.

SECTION I:

ABOUT THIS GUIDE

This guide was developed with many purposes in mind. First, it was designed to provide HR professionals with relevant information about the HR Certification Institute and its certification process. Second, it describes the Institute's practice-analysis process and its outcome—test specifications based on the PHR and SPHR Body of Knowledge. Third, it explains various ways to prepare for the PHR or SPHR exam. Finally, it provides sample test questions so individuals can assess their mastery of the PHR and SPHR Body of Knowledge.

There are two primary reasons HR professionals are reluctant to take the PHR and SPHR certification exams. First, there is fear of the unknown—not knowing what to study, for example, or what types of questions will be asked. Another reason is the fear of failure—not knowing one's level of proficiency before taking the exam. These two fears, whether real or imagined, prevent many capable HR professionals from taking one of the certification exams. This book was designed to alleviate those fears.

This publication is a starting point for formal training or informal self-development for HR professionals interested in individual or group study in the human resource management field.

Copies of the *HR Certification Institute's Official PHR® and SPHR® Certification Guide* may be purchased from the SHRMStore® by calling (800) 444-5006 or ordering online at www.shrmstore. shrm.org. In addition, this book can be purchased through Amazon and Barnes & Noble. Proceeds from the sales of this book are used to support the educational purposes and operations of the Institute. Inquiries about the certification program may be addressed to:

HR Certification Institute
1800 Duke Street
Alexandria, VA 22314
(866) 898-HRCI (4724)
+ 1 (703) 535-6000
TTY/TDD: (703) 548-6999
E-mail: info@hrci.org
Website: www.hrci.org

SECTION II:

HUMAN RESOURCE PROFESSIONALISM

In the mid-1960s, the American Society for Personnel Administration (now the Society for Human Resource Management) and Cornell University asked the U.S. Department of Labor a simple question: "What constitutes a profession?" The Department of Labor said there were five distinct characteristics that separate a profession from other pursuits or endeavors:

1. National Organization

A profession is defined by the existence of a national organization that can speak as a unified voice for its members and foster the development of the field. The Society for Human Resource Management (SHRM), with a membership exceeding 250,000, fulfills that role for the human resource management profession.

2. Code of Ethics

A profession has a code of ethics that identifies standards of behavior relating to fairness, justice, truthfulness and social responsibility. The HR Certification Institute's Code of Ethical and Professional Responsibility has been adopted to promote and maintain the highest standards of service and conduct for all persons it has recognized and certified to use any of its certification marks: PHR®, GPHR®, SPHR®, PHR-CA® and SPHR-CA®.

Those holding an HR Certification Institute credential commit to the following:

Professional Responsibility—As an HR Certification Institute certificant, you are responsible for adding value to the organizations you serve and contributing to the ethical success of those organizations. You accept professional responsibility for your individual decisions and actions. You are also an advocate for the HR profession by engaging in activities that enhance its credibility and value. You will:

1. Adhere to the highest standards of ethical and professional behavior.

2. Measure the effectiveness of HR in contributing to or achieving organizational goals.

3.   Comply with the law.

4.   Work consistently within the values of the profession.

5.   Strive to achieve the highest levels of service, performance and social responsibility.

6.   Advocate for the appropriate use and appreciation of human beings as employees.

7.   Advocate openly and within the established forums for debate in order to influence decision-making and results.

Professional Development—As an HR Certification Institute certificant, you must strive to meet the highest standards of competence and commit to strengthen your competencies on a continuous basis. You will:

1.   Commit to continuous learning, skills development and application of new knowledge related to both human resource management and the organizations you serve.

2.   Contribute to the body of knowledge, the evolution of the profession and the growth of individuals through teaching, research and dissemination of knowledge.

Ethical Leadership—As an HR Certification Institute certificant, you are expected to exhibit individual leadership as a role model for maintaining the highest standards of ethical conduct. You will:

1.   Be ethical and act ethically in every professional interaction.

2.   Question pending individual and group actions when necessary to ensure that decisions are ethical and are implemented in an ethical manner.

3.   Seek expert guidance if ever in doubt about the ethical propriety of a situation.

4.   Through teaching and mentoring, champion the development of others as ethical leaders in the profession and in organizations.

Fairness and Justice—As an HR Certification Institute certificant, you are ethically responsible for promoting and fostering fairness and justice for all employees and their organizations. You will:

1.   Respect the uniqueness and intrinsic worth of every individual.

2.   Treat people with dignity, respect and compassion to foster a trusting work environment free of harassment, intimidation and unlawful discrimination.

3.   Ensure that everyone has the opportunity to develop their skills and new competencies.

4. Assure an environment of inclusiveness and a commitment to diversity in the organizations you serve.

5. Develop, administer and advocate policies and procedures that foster fair, consistent and equitable treatment for all.

6. Regardless of personal interests, support decisions made by your organizations that are both ethical and legal.

7. Act in a responsible manner and practice sound management in the country or countries in which the organizations you serve operate.

Conflicts of Interest—As an HR Certification Institute certificant, you must maintain a high level of trust with our stakeholders. You must protect the interests of those stakeholders as well as your professional integrity and should not engage in activities that create actual, apparent or potential conflicts of interest. You will:

1. Adhere to and advocate the use of published policies on conflicts of interest within your organization.

2. Refrain from using your position for personal, material or financial gain or the appearance of such.

3. Refrain from giving or seeking preferential treatment in the human resources processes.

4. Prioritize your obligations to identify conflicts of interest or the appearance thereof. When conflicts arise, you will disclose them to relevant stakeholders.

Use of Information—As an HR Certification Institute certificant, you must consider and protect the rights of individuals, especially in the acquisition and dissemination of information while ensuring truthful communications and facilitating informed decision-making. You will:

1. Acquire and disseminate information through ethical and responsible means.

2. Ensure only appropriate information is used in decisions affecting the employment relationship.

3. Investigate the accuracy and source of information before allowing it to be used in employment-related decisions.

4. Maintain current and accurate HR information.

5. Safeguard restricted or confidential information.

6. Take appropriate steps to ensure the accuracy and completeness of all communicated information about HR policies and practices.

7. Take appropriate steps to ensure the accuracy and completeness of all communicated information used in HR-related training.

3. Research

Additionally, a profession is marked by the existence of applied research related to the field. The SHRM Foundation funds research into new and emerging areas of human resources. The HR Certification Institute provides financial support to the SHRM Foundation in its pursuit of advancing the HR field. In 2000, SHRM established a dedicated research department.

4. Body of Knowledge

A profession has a defined body of knowledge. The HR Certification Institute, through its practice analysis study, defines the PHR and SPHR Body of Knowledge. This body of knowledge (the basis of the PHR/SPHR test specifications) is disseminated to HR professionals through publications.

5. Credentialing

Lastly, a profession has a credentialing organization that sets professional standards in the field. The HR Certification Institute fulfills this requirement.

Together, SHRM, the SHRM Foundation and the HR Certification Institute meet the requirements that define the HR field as a profession. Although still developing, the high standards set by these organizations, combined with the high level of performance expected of an HR professional, will make the challenge of professionalism that much greater in the future.

THE HR CERTIFICATION INSTITUTE

The HR Certification Institute develops and maintains professional standards in the HR field. This is accomplished by defining and periodically updating the applicable HR body of knowledge, promoting the self-development of HR professionals, and recognizing and credentialing those who have met established experience requirements and have demonstrated mastery of the applicable HR body of knowledge by passing one of our exams.

The first certification exams were administered in the spring of 1976, following years of extensive work by a task force formed by SHRM. These efforts resulted in a certification program open to professionals in the HR field.

Today, the HR Certification Institute is governed by a volunteer board of directors composed of certified HR professionals and two to three public members. Item-writing, item-review and exam-review panels (also made up of volunteers) write test questions, review test specifications and bibliographic reference lists, and review exam forms. The Institute employs a highly qualified staff to administer its certification program.

PHR AND SPHR CERTIFICATION

The HR Certification Institute offers two exams developed for HR professionals responsible for U.S. HR issues—the PHR® exam and SPHR® exam. In addition, in 2007 we began offering a California state-specific credential for certified PHRs and SPHRs who practice HR in California. We also offer an exam developed for HR professionals with cross-border HR responsibilities—the Global Professional in Human Resources (GPHR) exam. (Note that this guide was developed only for the PHR and SPHR exams. Please see the *HR Certification Institute's Official GPHR® Certification Guide* for information on that exam.)

The following chart summarizes the minimum eligibility requirements that a candidate for certification must meet:

PHR ELIGIBILITY	SPHR ELIGIBILITY
1 year of demonstrated professional (exempt-level) HR experience with a master's degree or higher	4 years of demonstrated professional (exempt-level) HR experience with a master's degree or higher
2 years of demonstrated professional (exempt-level) HR experience with a bachelor's degree	5 years of demonstrated professional (exempt-level) HR experience with a bachelor's degree
4 years of demonstrated professional (exempt-level) HR experience with less than a bachelor's degree	7 years of demonstrated professional (exempt-level) HR experience with less than a bachelor's degree

The PHR® exam focuses more on the technical and operational aspects of human resources. The SPHR® exam focuses on strategic HR policy issues.

Candidates should select the certification exam level that they feel best represents their mastery of the PHR and SPHR Body of Knowledge. Candidate performance has shown that appropriate professional (exempt-level) HR work experience and educational background contribute significantly to the likelihood of success on the exams. Success depends on mastery of the entire body of knowledge as reflected in the test specifications. Therefore, candidates should carefully assess their qualifications before selecting the certification exam level.

The PHR and SPHR exams assess generalist knowledge of the U.S. HR field, including business management and strategy, workforce planning and employment, HR development, compensation and benefits, employee and labor relations, and risk management. The SPHR exam supersedes the PHR designation. This means that the PHR and SPHR exams cannot be held at the same time.

CHOOSING THE RIGHT EXAM LEVEL

An honest assessment of skills, knowledge and responsibilities within the HR function is critical when deciding which exam to take. The following profiles of typical PHR and SPHR candidates may help you decide which level is right for you.

THE IDEAL **PHR** CANDIDATE GENERALLY:	THE IDEAL **SPHR** CANDIDATE GENERALLY:
• Focuses on program implementation.	• Designs and plans rather than implements.
• Has tactical/logistical orientation.	• Focuses on the "big picture."
• Has accountability to another HR professional within the organization.	• Has ultimate accountability in the HR department.
• Possesses two to four years of professional (exempt-level) generalist HR work experience, but because of career length, may lack the breadth and depth of a more senior-level generalist.	• Possesses six to eight years of progressive HR experience.
	• Has the breadth and depth of HR generalist knowledge.
• Has not had progressive HR work experience by virtue of career length or specialization.	• Uses judgment obtained with time and application of knowledge.
	• Is not specialized, but has a generalist role within the organization.
• Focuses his or her effect on the organization within the HR department, rather than organizationwide.	• Understands the effect of decisions within and outside of the organization.
• Commands respect through the credibility of knowledge and the use of policies and guidelines to make decisions.	• Understands the business, not just the HR function.
	• Manages relationships and has influence within the overall organization.
	• Commands credibility within the organization, community and field through experience.

THE HR CERTIFICATION INSTITUTE ASSESSMENT EXAMS

The HR Certification Institute offers online assessment exams for both the PHR® and SPHR® exams. Potential candidates can use these exams to assess their knowledge level before taking the actual exam and/or to measure the results of their test preparation activities. The assessment exams were developed using actual retired test questions from previous exams and will give candidates a chance to become familiar with the format of the exam questions and determine their readiness for the actual exam. Before registering for the exam, consider investing in an assessment exam. For more information, visit the "Assessments & Preparation" section of www.hrci.org

DEFINITIONS

The PHR and SPHR exams are developed for HR professionals who are currently working at a professional (exempt) level in the HR field. While that work need not always be exclusively in human resources, the majority (51 percent) of a person's daily activities must be within the HR function, or the individual must have direct supervision of those who deliver HR services.

Therefore, the following general definitions apply when assessing eligibility:

- Practitioner: One whose duties are those normally found in the typical HR function.
- Educator: One whose principal area of instruction is in the HR field in an accredited institution of higher education.
- Researcher: One whose research activities are restricted primarily to the HR field.
- Consultant: One whose consulting activities are predominantly in the HR field.

USE OF CERTIFICATION

Our certifications are voluntary and conferred by the HR Certification Institute solely when an HR professional has demonstrated achievement of national standards by passing the PHR, SPHR, PHR-CA/SPHR-CA or GPHR exam. Persons or organizations choosing to incorporate PHR, SPHR, GPHR or PHR-CA/SPHR-CA certification as a condition of employment or advancement do so of their own volition. Candidates must determine for themselves whether the use of such a certification process, including its eligibility and recertification requirements (when coupled with other requirements imposed by such persons), meets their needs and complies with applicable laws.

APPLYING FOR THE EXAMS

To apply for the PHR or SPHR exam, please visit www.hrci.org. For complete information about how to apply for the exams, please review the *Certification Handbook*. This handbook, updated annually, provides information about the certification process and eligibility requirements. In addition, it includes the current exam fee schedule and test dates/deadlines. You may download a copy of the handbook at www.hrci.org under the "Resources" section.

Candidates should refer only to the most recent handbook, as the HR Certification Institute may change or modify policies and procedures annually.

PHR AND SPHR RECERTIFICATION

PHR or SPHR certification demonstrates mastery of the U.S. HR body of knowledge in an increasingly demanding field. As every HR professional knows, however, the field is in flux. HR professionals who strive to maintain their professional edge must keep up with the rapid change and new dimensions that define the profession. Recertification demonstrates that certified professionals have stayed current with changes and updated their HR knowledge.

Recertification is required within three years of passing the exam, and each subsequent recertification period is for three years. There are two ways to recertify:

Recertification by Exam

All requirements for recertification may be met by passing the current, applicable exam. Candidates who select this option must take the exam at the same designation level before their certification cycle expires. For more information about this method of recertification, please visit www.hrci.org and access the "Recertification" section.

Recertification by Updating Education and Experience

Recertification through professional development and experience can be achieved by accumulating 60 credit hours during a recertification cycle. Credit hours can be achieved through a variety of methods. SPHR-certified professionals are required to earn 15 of the 60 recertification credit hours specifically in the business management and strategy functional area. These recertification credit hours can be acquired through the continuing education, instruction, on-the-job or research/publishing categories. Please refer to the latest recertification handbook and application (distributed by the HR Certification Institute or available at www.hrci.org) for more information on the number of credit hours allowed per category and per designation.

Continuing Education: Recertification credit can be earned by participating in HR-related courses, workshops, seminars or conferences. All 60 recertification credit hours can be obtained in this category. (Note: A maximum of 20 recertification credit hours can be accumulated through passive learning methods such as video conferences, audiotapes and webcasts over a three-year period.)

Research and/or Publishing: Recertification credit can be earned by conducting an HR-related research project or by writing and publishing in the HR field. Writing an article for a newsletter will not meet this requirement. A maximum of 20 recertification credit hours can be obtained in this category.

Instruction/Teaching: Recertification candidates can earn credit hours by preparing for and teaching a new HR college-level class or making a presentation at a workshop or conference (including formal in-house training programs). Credits can be earned only for the first time the presentation is made. A maximum of 20 recertification credit hours can be obtained in this category.

On-the-Job: Certain work-related projects can earn recertification credit. A first-time work activity that adds to the candidate's HR knowledge base can be credited. The focus in this area is to capture new knowledge. A maximum of 20 recertification credit hours can be obtained in this category.

Leadership: HR professionals can earn recertification credit hours through leadership responsibilities in an HR professional organization at a national, area, state or local level, or in a civic/community activity where HR knowledge is the primary reason for the affiliation. A maximum of 10 recertification credit hours can be obtained in this category.

Professional Membership: As many as 10 recertification credit hours (during a three-year recertification cycle) are available for professionals who are members of a national or international HR organization.

RECERTIFICATION APPLICATION AND FEES

All certified HR professionals have an online file in which they can record their recertification activities. Information on recertification fees and how to access this online file can be found in the *Recertification Handbook* in the "Resources" section of www.hrci.org.

SECTION III:

THE PHR AND SPHR BODY OF KNOWLEDGE

DEFINING THE PHR AND SPHR BODY OF KNOWLEDGE

What should an HR practitioner know—and be able to apply—to be considered a competent HR generalist? This is the fundamental question the HR Certification Institute seeks to answer through its practice analysis study, an extensive research program specifically designed to define and update an HR body of knowledge.

The HR field is dynamic and constantly changing. Consequently, the knowledge requirements must reflect these changes. The practice analysis process keeps HR knowledge requirements both relevant and contemporary.

To set standards for the credentialing of a profession, the relevant body of knowledge must first be defined. The PHR and SPHR Body of Knowledge is the foundation upon which our PHR and SPHR certification program is built. From this body of knowledge, test specifications are developed. In turn, these specifications are used as a blueprint for the PHR and SPHR exams. Exam items are developed to measure the knowledge requirements that reflect the topics in the test specifications.

The end result of this research is a set of assurances that PHR and SPHR certifications are:
- Based on a set of well-defined knowledge requirements.
- Current and able to respond to rapid changes in the field.
- Based on "real-life" human resource management practices.
- Focused on important knowledge and not trivial matters.

Codification research to define the PHR and SPHR Body of Knowledge began in 1976 with a group of U.S. HR professionals. Their roles were to critique draft test specifications and weightings, recommend revisions, suggest sources for bibliographies and make other pertinent comments.

To revise the test specifications, a modified Delphi technique involving hundreds of professionals was used in 1979 and in 1984. This method used a multiple-nomination technique to identify experts who were widely known and respected as HR leaders. These experts included practitioners, educators, researchers and consultants. They were asked to perform a highly detailed evaluation of the test specifications and bibliographies. Statistical analyses were performed. The resulting body of knowledge represented the consensus views of those experts.

Before 1988, the practice analysis methodology used HR experts for a normative (or what the field ought to be) perspective. In 1988, the HR Certification Institute (then known as the Personnel Accreditation Institute) went to the "real" experts in the HR field for a descriptive ("the way it is") perspective. More than 41,000 HR practitioners, educators, researchers and consultants received a detailed questionnaire of 234 separate items. Participants were asked to evaluate each of the questions in terms of how essential it was to their particular job. In addition, a number of demographic factors were asked to allow for more in-depth analyses of data.

The HR Certification Institute board and SHRM committee chairs gathered the data from the questionnaire. That data was then compiled into a comprehensive content outline that served as the foundation for the 1988 HR Certification Institute test specifications.

The HR Certification Institute periodically undergoes equally extensive processes and updates the test specifications. In 2010 the HR Certification Institute conducted a study to validate current HR practices and the PHR and SPHR test specifications. Results of this study will be reflected in the exams beginning with those administered in May/June 2012.

To verify and revise test specifications between major surveys, the HR Certification Institute uses expert reviews, extensive literature searches and analyses of HR textbooks. This kind of environmental scan identifies new knowledge requirements, as well as those that may be obsolete. The current test specifications are the basis for certification testing and can be found in these publications/products (this is not an exhaustive list):

- *HR Certification Institute's Certification Handbook*
- *The Official PHR and SPHR Certification Guide*
- www.hrci.org

The PHR and SPHR Body of Knowledge is constantly changing. Consequently, the HR Certification Institute's research ensures that the test specifications and exams reflect current HR knowledge and practices.

PHR AND SPHR TEST SPECIFICATIONS

The PHR and SPHR exams are divided into functional areas. The weighting of each area is based on its relative importance to the knowledge requirements of an HR generalist. The PHR and SPHR exams are weighted accordingly:

	PHR	SPHR
Business Management and Strategy	11%	30%
Workforce Planning and Employment	24%	17%
Human Resource Development	18%	19%
Compensation and Benefits	19%	13%
Employee and Labor Relations	20%	14%
Risk Management	8%	7%

The numbers in parentheses below indicate the percentage composition on both exams for each major functional area. The first number is the PHR percentage; the second number is the SPHR percentage.

If a responsibility is marked "PHR only" or "SPHR only," it means that during the practice analysis, it was performed mainly by one OR the other level of HR professional. Questions on that particular responsibility will appear on the exam that is indicated.

FUNCTIONAL AREA 01:
BUSINESS MANAGEMENT & STRATEGY (11%, 30%)

Developing, contributing to and supporting the organization's mission, vision, values, strategic goals and objectives; formulating policies; guiding and leading the change process; and evaluating organizational effectiveness as an organizational leader.

Responsibilities:

01 Interpret and apply information related to the organization's operations from internal sources, including finance, accounting, business development, marketing, sales, operations and information technology, in order to contribute to the development of the organization's strategic plan.

02   Interpret information from external sources related to the general business environment, industry practices and developments, technological advances, economic environment, labor force, and the legal and regulatory environment, in order to contribute to the development of the organization's strategic plan.

03   Participate as a contributing partner in the organization's strategic planning process (for example: provide and lead workforce planning discussion with management, develop and present long-term forecast of human capital needs at the organizational level). **SPHR only**

04   Establish strategic relationships with key individuals in the organization to influence organizational decision-making.

05   Establish relationships/alliances with key individuals and outside organizations to assist in achieving the organization's strategic goals and objectives (for example: corporate social responsibility and community partnership).

06   Develop and utilize business metrics to measure the achievement of the organization's strategic goals and objectives (for example: key performance indicators, balanced scorecard). **SPHR only**

07   Develop, influence and execute strategies for managing organizational change that balance the expectations and needs of the organization, its employees and other stakeholders.

08   Develop and align the human resource strategic plan with the organization's strategic plan. **SPHR only**

09   Facilitate the development and communication of the organization's core values, vision, mission and ethical behaviors.

10   Reinforce the organization's core values and behavioral expectations through modeling, communication and coaching.

11   Provide data such as human capital projections and costs that support the organization's overall budget.

12   Develop and execute business plans (i.e., annual goals and objectives) that correlate with the organization's strategic plan's performance expectations to include growth targets, new programs/services and net income expectations. **SPHR only**

13   Perform cost/benefit analyses on proposed projects. **SPHR only**

14   Develop and manage an HR budget that supports the organization's strategic goals, objectives and values. **SPHR only**

15   Monitor the legislative and regulatory environment for proposed changes and their potential impact on the organization, taking appropriate proactive steps to support, modify or oppose the proposed changes.

16   Develop policies and procedures to support corporate governance initiatives (for example: whistleblower protection, code of ethics). **SPHR only**

17   Participate in enterprise risk management by ensuring that policies contribute to protecting the organization from potential risks.

18   Identify and evaluate alternatives and recommend strategies for vendor selection and/ or outsourcing. **SPHR only**

19   Oversee or lead the transition and/or implementation of new systems, service centers and outsourcing. **SPHR only**

20 Participate in strategic decision-making and due diligence activities related to organizational structure and design (for example: corporate restructuring, mergers and acquisitions, divestitures). **SPHR only**

21 Determine strategic application of integrated technical tools and systems (for example: new enterprise software, performance management tools, self-service technologies). **SPHR only**

Knowledge of:

01 The organization's mission, vision, values, business goals, objectives, plans and processes.

02 Legislative and regulatory processes.

03 Strategic planning process, design, implementation and evaluation.

04 Management functions, including planning, organizing, directing and controlling.

05 Corporate governance procedures and compliance (for example: Sarbanes-Oxley Act).

06 Due diligence processes (for example: M&A, divestitures). **SPHR only**

07 Transition techniques for corporate restructuring, M&A, offshoring and divestitures. **SPHR only**

08 Elements of a cost-benefit analysis during the life cycle of the business (such as scenarios for growth, including expected, economic stressed and worst-case conditions) and the impact on net worth/earnings for short-, mid- and long-term horizons.

09 Business concepts (for example: competitive advantage, organizational branding, business case development, corporate responsibility).

10 Business processes (for example: operations, sales and marketing, data management).

FUNCTIONAL AREA 02:
WORKFORCE PLANNING AND EMPLOYMENT (24%, 17%)

Developing, implementing and evaluating sourcing, recruitment, hiring, orientation, succession planning, retention and organizational exit programs necessary to ensure the workforce's ability to achieve the organization's goals and objectives.

Responsibilities:

01 Ensure that workforce planning and employment activities are compliant with applicable federal laws and regulations.

02 Identify workforce requirements to achieve the organization's short- and long-term goals and objectives (for example: corporate restructuring, workforce expansion or reduction).

03 Conduct job analyses to create and/or update job descriptions and identify job competencies.

04 Identify, review, document and update essential job functions for positions.

05 Influence and establish criteria for hiring, retaining and promoting based on job descriptions and required competencies.

06   Analyze labor market for trends that affect the ability to meet workforce requirements (for example: federal/state data reports).

07   Assess skill sets of internal workforce and external labor market to determine the availability of qualified candidates, utilizing third-party vendors or agencies as appropriate.

08   Identify internal and external recruitment sources (for example: employee referrals, diversity groups, social media) and implement selected recruitment methods.

09   Establish metrics for workforce planning (for example: recruitment and turnover statistics, costs).

10   Brand and market the organization to potential qualified applicants.

11   Develop and implement selection procedures (for example: applicant tracking, interviewing, reference and background checking).

12   Develop and extend employment offers and conduct negotiations as necessary.

13   Administer post-offer employment activities (for example: execute employment agreements, complete I-9/e-Verify process, coordinate relocations and immigration).

14   Develop, implement and evaluate orientation and onboarding processes for new hires, rehires and transfers.

15   Develop, implement and evaluate employee retention strategies and practices.

16   Develop, implement and evaluate the succession planning process. **SPHR only**

17   Develop and implement the organizational exit/offboarding process for both voluntary and involuntary terminations, including planning for reductions in force (RIF).

18   Develop, implement and evaluate an affirmative action plan (AAP) as required.

19   Develop and implement a record retention process for handling documents and employee files (for example: pre-employment files, medical files, benefits files).

Knowledge of:

11   Applicable federal laws and regulations related to workforce planning and employment activities (for example: Title VII, ADA, EEOC Uniform Guidelines on Employee Selection Procedures, Immigration Reform and Control Act).

12   Methods to assess past and future staffing effectiveness (for example: costs-per-hire, selection ratios, adverse impact).

13   Recruitment sources (for example: employee referral, social networking/social media) for targeting passive, semi-active and active candidates.

14   Recruitment strategies.

15   Staffing alternatives (for example: outsourcing, job sharing, phased retirement).

16   Planning techniques (for example: succession planning, forecasting).

17   Reliability and validity of selection tests/tools/methods.

18   Use and interpretation of selection tests (for example: psychological/personality, cognitive, motor/physical assessments, performance, assessment center).

19   Interviewing techniques (for example: behavioral, situational, panel).

20   Impact of compensation and benefits on recruitment and retention.

21   International HR and implications of global workforce for workforce planning and employment. **SPHR only**

22   Voluntary and involuntary terminations, downsizing, restructuring, and outplacement strategies and practices.

23   Internal workforce assessment techniques (for example: skills testing, skills inventory, workforce demographic analysis).

24   Employment policies, practices and procedures (for example: orientation, onboarding, retention).

25   Employer marketing and branding techniques.

26   Negotiation skills and techniques.

FUNCTIONAL AREA 03:
HUMAN RESOURCE DEVELOPMENT (18%, 19%)

Developing, implementing and evaluating activities and programs that address employee training and development, performance appraisal, and talent and performance management to ensure that the knowledge, skills, abilities and performance of the workforce meet current and future organizational and individual needs.

Responsibilities:

01   Ensure that human resource development activities are compliant with all applicable federal laws and regulations.

02   Conduct a needs assessment to identify and establish priorities regarding human resource development activities.

03   Develop/select and implement employee training programs (for example: leadership skills, harassment prevention, computer skills) to increase individual and organizational effectiveness.

04   Evaluate effectiveness of employee training programs through the use of metrics (for example: participant surveys, pre- and post-testing). **SPHR only**

05   Develop, implement and evaluate talent management programs that include assessing talent, developing career paths and managing the placement of high-potential employees.

06   Develop, select and evaluate performance appraisal processes (for example: instruments, ranking and rating scales) to increase individual and organizational effectiveness.

07   Develop, implement and evaluate performance management programs and procedures (includes training for evaluators).

08   Develop/select, implement and evaluate programs (for example: telecommuting, diversity initiatives, repatriation) to meet the changing needs of employees and the organization. **SPHR only**

09   Provide coaching to managers and executives regarding effectively managing organizational talent.

Knowledge of:

27   Applicable federal laws and regulations related to human resource development activities (for example: Title VII, ADA, Title 17 [Copyright law]).

28   Career development and leadership development theories and applications (for example: succession planning, dual career ladders).

29   Organizational development (OD) theories and applications.

30   Training program development techniques to create general and specialized training programs.

31   Facilitation techniques, instructional methods and program delivery mechanisms.

32   Task/process analysis.

33   Performance appraisal methods (for example: instruments, ranking and rating scales).

34   Performance management methods (for example: goal setting, relationship to compensation, job placements/promotions).

35   Applicable global issues (for example: international law, culture, local management approaches/practices, societal norms). **SPHR only**

36   Techniques to assess training program effectiveness, including use of applicable metrics (for example: participant surveys, pre- and post-testing).

37   Mentoring and executive coaching.

FUNCTIONAL AREA 04:
COMPENSATION AND BENEFITS (19%, 13%)

Developing/selecting, implementing/administering and evaluating compensation and benefits programs for all employee groups in order to support the organization's goals, objectives and values.

Responsibilities

01   Ensure that compensation and benefits programs are compliant with applicable federal laws and regulations.

02   Develop, implement and evaluate compensation policies/programs (for example: pay structures, performance-based pay, internal and external equity).

03   Manage payroll-related information (for example: new hires, adjustments, terminations).

04   Manage outsourced compensation and benefits components (for example: payroll vendors, COBRA administration, employee recognition vendors). **PHR only**

05   Conduct compensation and benefits programs needs assessments (for example: benchmarking, employee surveys, trend analysis).

06   Develop/select, implement/administer, update and evaluate benefits programs (for example: health and welfare, wellness, retirement, stock purchase).

07   Communicate and train the workforce in the compensation and benefits programs, policies and processes (for example: self-service technologies).

08   Develop/select, implement/administer, update and evaluate an ethically sound executive compensation program (for example: stock options, bonuses, supplemental retirement plans). **SPHR only**

09   Develop, implement/administer and evaluate expatriate and foreign national compensation and benefits programs. **SPHR only**

Knowledge of:

38   Applicable federal laws and regulations related to compensation, benefits and tax (for example: FLSA, ERISA, FMLA, USERRA).

39   Compensation and benefits strategies.

40   Budgeting and accounting practices related to compensation and benefits.

41   Job evaluation methods.

42   Job pricing and pay structures.

43   External labor markets and/or economic factors.

44   Pay programs (for example: variable, merit).

45   Executive compensation methods. **SPHR only**

46   Noncash compensation methods (for example: equity programs, noncash rewards).

47   Benefits programs (for example: health and welfare, retirement, employee assistance programs [EAPs])

48   International compensation laws and practices (for example: expatriate compensation, entitlements, choice of law codes). **SPHR only**

49   Fiduciary responsibilities related to compensation and benefits.

FUNCTIONAL AREA 05:
EMPLOYEE AND LABOR RELATIONS (20%, 14%)

Developing, implementing/administering and evaluating the workplace in order to maintain relationships and working conditions that balance employer/employee needs and rights in support of the organization's goals and objectives.

Responsibilities

01   Ensure that employee and labor relations activities are compliant with applicable federal laws and regulations.

02   Assess organizational climate by obtaining employee input (for example: focus groups, employee surveys, staff meetings).

03   Develop and implement employee relations programs (for example: recognition, special events, diversity programs) that promote a positive organizational culture.

04   Evaluate effectiveness of employee relations programs through the use of metrics (for example: exit interviews, employee surveys, turnover rates).

05   Establish, update and communicate workplace policies and procedures (for example: employee handbook, reference guides or standard operating procedures) and monitor their application and enforcement to ensure consistency.

06   Develop and implement a discipline policy based on organizational code of conduct/ ethics, ensuring that no disparate impact or other legal issues arise.

07   Create and administer a termination process (for example: reductions in force, policy violations, poor performance) ensuring that no disparate impact or other legal issues arise.

08   Develop, administer and evaluate grievance/dispute resolution and performance improvement policies and procedures.

09   Investigate and resolve employee complaints filed with federal agencies involving employment practices or working conditions, utilizing professional resources as necessary (for example: legal counsel, mediation/arbitration specialists, investigators).

10   Develop and direct proactive employee relations strategies for remaining union-free in non-organized locations. **SPHR only**

11   Direct and/or participate in collective bargaining activities, including contract negotiation, costing and administration.

Knowledge of:

50   Applicable federal laws affecting employment in union and nonunion environments, such as laws regarding antidiscrimination policies, sexual harassment, labor relations and privacy (for example: WARN Act, Title VII, NLRA).

51   Techniques and tools for facilitating positive employee relations (for example: employee surveys, dispute/conflict resolution, labor/management cooperative strategies).

52   Employee involvement strategies (for example: employee management committees, self-directed work teams, staff meetings).

53   Individual employment rights issues and practices (for example: employment at will, negligent hiring, defamation).

54   Workplace behavior issues/practices (for example: absenteeism and performance improvement).

55   Unfair labor practices.

56   The collective bargaining process, strategies and concepts (for example: contract negotiation, costing and administration).

57   Legal disciplinary procedures.

58   Positive employee relations strategies and nonmonetary rewards.

59   Techniques for conducting unbiased investigations.

60   Legal termination procedures.

FUNCTIONAL AREA 06:
RISK MANAGEMENT (8%, 7%)

Developing, implementing/administering and evaluating programs, procedures and policies in order to provide a safe, secure working environment and to protect the organization from potential liability.

Responsibilities

01 Ensure that workplace health, safety, security and privacy activities are compliant with applicable federal laws and regulations.

02 Conduct a needs analysis to identify the organization's safety requirements.

03 Develop/select and implement/administer occupational injury and illness prevention programs (for example: OSHA, workers' compensation). **PHR only**

04 Establish and administer a return-to-work process after illness or injury to ensure a safe workplace (for example: modified duty assignment, reasonable accommodations, independent medical exam).

05 Develop/select, implement and evaluate plans and policies to protect employees and other individuals, and to minimize the organization's loss and liability (for example: emergency response, workplace violence, substance abuse).

06 Communicate and train the workforce on security plans and policies.

07 Develop, monitor and test business continuity and disaster recovery plans.

08 Communicate and train the workforce on the business continuity and disaster recovery plans.

09 Develop policies and procedures to direct the appropriate use of electronic media and hardware (for example: e-mail, social media and appropriate website access).

10 Develop and administer internal and external privacy policies (for example: identity theft, data protection, workplace monitoring).

Knowledge of:

61 Applicable federal laws and regulations related to workplace health, safety, security and privacy (for example: OSHA, Drug-Free Workplace Act, ADA, HIPAA, Sarbanes-Oxley Act).

62 Occupational injury and illness prevention (safety) and compensation programs.

63 Investigation procedures of workplace safety, health and security enforcement agencies.

64 Return to work procedures (for example: interactive dialog, job modification, accommodations).

65 Workplace safety risks (for example: trip hazards, blood-borne pathogens).

66 Workplace security risks (for example: theft, corporate espionage, sabotage).

67 Potential violent behavior and workplace violence conditions.

68 General health and safety practices (for example: evacuation, hazard communication, ergonomic evaluations).

69 Organizational incident and emergency response plans.

70 Internal investigation, monitoring and surveillance techniques.

71 Employer/employee rights related to substance abuse.

72 Business continuity and disaster recovery plans (for example: data storage and backup, alternative work locations, procedures).

73 Data integrity techniques and technology (for example: data sharing, password usage, social engineering).

74 Technology and applications (for example: social media, monitoring software, biometrics).

75 Financial management practices (for example: procurement policies, credit card policies and guidelines, expense policies).

Core Knowledge

76 Needs assessment and analysis.

77 Third-party or vendor selection, contract negotiation and management, including development of requests for proposals (RFPs).

78 Communication skills and strategies (for example: presentation, collaboration, sensitivity).

79 Organizational documentation requirements to meet federal and state guidelines.

80 Adult learning processes.

81 Motivation concepts and applications.

82 Training techniques (for example: virtual, classroom, on-the-job).

83 Leadership concepts and applications.

84 Project management concepts and applications.

85 Diversity concepts and applications (for example: generational, cultural competency, learning styles).

86 Human relations concepts and applications (for example: emotional intelligence, organizational behavior).

87 Ethical and professional standards.

88 Technology to support HR activities (for example: HR information systems, employee self-service, e-learning, applicant tracking systems).

89 Qualitative and quantitative methods and tools for analysis, interpretation and decision-making purposes (for example: metrics and measurements, cost/benefit analysis, financial statement analysis).

90 Change management theory, methods and application.

91 Job analysis and job description methods.

92 Employee records management (for example: electronic/paper, retention, disposal).

93 Techniques for forecasting, planning and predicting the impact of HR activities and programs across functional areas.

94 Types of organizational structures (for example: matrix, hierarchy).

95 Environmental scanning concepts and applications (for example: strengths, weaknesses, opportunities and threats [SWOT], and political, economic, social and technological [PEST]).

96 Methods for assessing employee attitudes, opinions and satisfaction (for example: surveys, focus groups/panels).

97 Budgeting, accounting and financial concepts.

98 Risk-management techniques.

RESOURCES

The following selected resources, categorized by functional areas, may help you prepare for the PHR or SPHR exam. This is not an exhaustive list of resources; rather, it represents a solid foundation for an HR professional library.

Business Management and Strategy

- Cascio, W. F., & Boudreau, J. W. (2009). *Investing in people: Financial impact of human resource initiatives.* New Jersey: FT Press.

- Cascio, W. F. (2009). *Managing human resources* (8th ed.). New York: McGraw-Hill Companies.

- DeCenzo, D. A., & Robbins, S. P. (2009). *Fundamentals of human resource management* (10th ed.). New York: John Wiley & Sons.

- Fitz-Enz, J. (2009). *The ROI of human capital: Measuring the economic value of human performance.* New York: AMACOM.

- Goldsmith, M., Effron, M., & Gandossy, R. (2003). *Human resources in the 21st century.* New York: John Wiley & Sons.

- Greer, C. R. (2000). *Strategic human resource management.* New Jersey: Prentice Hall.

- Lawler, E. E., Worley, C. G., & Creelman, D. (2011). *Management reset: Organizing for sustainable effectiveness.* San Francisco: Jossey-Bass.

- Phillips, J. J., & Phillips, P. P. (2005). *Proving the value of HR: How and why to measure ROI.* Alexandria, VA: Society for Human Resource Management.

Workforce Planning and Employment

- Alhrichs, N. S. (2000). *Competing for talent: Key recruitment and retention strategies for becoming an employer of choice.* Palo Alto, CA: Consulting Psychologists Press.

- Fitz-enz, J. (2009). *The ROI of human capital: Measuring the economic value of employee performance.* New York, NY: AMACOM.

Human Resource Development

- Federman, B. (2009). *Employee engagement: A roadmap for creating profits, optimizing performance, and increasing loyalty.* New York, NY: Pfeiffer.

- Luthans, F., Youssef, C. M., & Avolio, B. J. (2006). *Psychological capital: Developing the human competitive edge.* New York: Oxford University Press.

- Phillips, J. J., & Connell, A. O. (2003). *Managing employee retention: A strategic accountability approach.* Burlington, MA: Butterworth-Heinemann, and Alexandria, VA: Society for Human Resource Management.

- Russ-Eft, D., & Preskill, H. (2009). *Evaluation in organizations: A systematic approach to enhancing learning, performance, and change.* Philadelphia, PA: Basic Books.

Compensation and Benefits

- Berger, L. A., & Berger, D. (2008). *The compensation handbook: The state-of-the-art guide to compensation strategy & design* (5th ed.). New York: McGraw Hill.

- Henderson, R. I. (2005). *Compensation management in a knowledge-based world* (10th ed.). New Jersey: Prentice Hall.

- Lawler, E. (2000). *Rewarding excellence: Pay strategies for the new economy.* San Francisco: Jossey-Bass Inc.

- WorldatWork. (2007). *The WorldatWork handbook of compensation, benefits & total rewards: A comprehensive guide for HR professionals.* Hoboken, NJ: John Wiley & Sons.

Employee and Labor Relations

- BNA. (2007). *Grievance guide* (12th ed.). Arlington, VA: BNA Books.

- Carrell, M., & Heavrin, C. (2009). *Labor relations and collective bargaining cases, practice and law* (9th ed.). New Jersey: Prentice Hall.

- Holley, W., Jennings, K. M., & Wolters, R. S. (2008). *The labor relations process.* Mason, OH: South-Western Cengage Learning.

Risk Management

- Buckley, J. F. (2010). *State by state guide to workplace safety regulation 2011.* New York: Wolters Kluwer Law & Business.

- Hopwood, D. & Thompson, S. (2006). *Workplace safety: A guide for small and midsized companies.* Hoboken, NJ: John Wiley & Sons.

- Milam-Perez, L. A. (2003). *HR how-to: Workplace safety.* New York: Wolters Kluwer Law & Business.

General Human Resource Management

- Dessler, G. (2010). *Human resource management* (12th ed.). New Jersey: Prentice Hall

- Mathis, R. L., & Jackson, J. L. (2011). *Human resource management* (13th ed.). United States: South-Western College Publishing.

- Society for Human Resource Management. (2011). *SHRM learning system.* Alexandria, VA: Society for Human Resource Management.

SECTION IV:

PHR AND SPHR CERTIFICATION EXAMS

The Institute's PHR and SPHR certification exams are offered by computer during two eight-week exam periods at more than 250 Prometric testing centers throughout the United States, U.S. territories and Canada. In addition, Prometric has test center locations worldwide. Beginning in 2012, both exams will consist of 175 multiple-choice questions, each with four possible answers. Of the 175 questions, 25 are pre-test questions not counted in the scoring of the exam; instead, they are used for statistical purposes. Three hours are allotted to complete the exam. A passing (or cut) score is determined using the expert judgments of a standards-setting panel. This score will vary depending on the actual exam form used.

The exams measure mastery of the PHR and SPHR Body of Knowledge. Both exams cover the same functional areas but differ in terms of the individual test items and the functional area's percentage weightings. Preparation for the exam is best accomplished by mastering the application of the PHR and SPHR Body of Knowledge.

The HR Certification Institute uses multiple-choice exams because they:
- Are flexible and adaptable.
- Tend to be more reliable than other formats.
- Can accommodate a wide range of skills, knowledge and abilities to be measured.
- Provide a good sampling.
- Have low chance scores.
- Can be machine-scored.

Multiple-choice items consist of three parts:
1. Stem: The stem states the problem or question to be answered.
2. Correct answer: The correct answer is one of four potential options and represents the only correct response or best correct response. "Best" means a panel of subject matter experts would agree to this judgment.
3. Distractors: The remaining options are distractors and are incorrect responses. They are plausible, yet wrong or not the best possible answer.

The following is an example of the parts of a multiple-choice item:

Stem: Typically, the most unreliable tool used in the selection process is a(n):

Correct answer:	**a. Employment interview.**
Distractor:	b. Selection test.
Distractor:	c. Physical exam.
Distractor:	d. Background check.

All exam questions are written by certified HR professionals. These important volunteers serve on one of two HR Certification Institute Item Writing Panels and are given extensive training and specific guidelines on item development.

Exam questions (or items) go through an exhaustive item-review process. A separate group of certified HR professionals (Item Review Panel) thoroughly scrutinizes each item and perform a number of validity checks. Each remaining item is then categorized as either a PHR or SPHR item and coded to the Institute's test specifications. Once the Item Review Panel approves an item, it is eligible to be pre-tested on an exam form to ensure that it meets the statistical criteria to establish its reliability and link to the established test specifications.

A third group of HR professionals—the Exam Review Panel—reviews and approves each exam form before use.

This multi-step process of item development, item review, exam review and pre-testing ensures that items are:

- Clear, unambiguous and grammatically correct.

- Technically correct.

- Appropriate in terms of fairness—geographically, ethnically or culturally.

- Important for HR professionals to know.

- Correctly coded to the HR Certification Institute test specifications. The PHR and SPHR exams differ significantly in terms of the weight assigned to each of the functional areas. Of equal importance is the difference in focus and format of the individual questions on the exams. In general, PHR questions are more technical application questions. Many are at the operational level. On the other hand, SPHR questions tend to be more policy application questions. Many of the questions are at the strategic level. In addition, there is a greater proportion of scenario questions on the SPHR exam. A scenario question poses an HR situation followed by a series of questions based on the information supplied. Scenario questions are particularly well suited to SPHR examinees because they represent typical situations that senior-level HR practitioners encounter and the diverse knowledge requirements needed to solve those situations.

The exams are administered through a professional testing service. This organization supplies expert counsel in exam design, construction and administration, and provides analysis of exam results.

EXAM PREPARATION METHODS, STRATEGIES AND RESOURCES

Exam preparation is an important issue for candidates. There are a number of study methods available for the exams; selecting a method is a matter of individual preference based on what best fits into one's life and learning style. Methods range from the highly informal individual self-study to highly structured courses and workshops.

The strategy used to prepare for the PHR or SPHR exam is equally important. Just as world-class athletes must peak at the precise moment of competition, so must candidates on exam day. In addition to being able to master the PHR and SPHR Body of Knowledge, candidates should be mentally and physically prepared to take the exam. Strategy is a critical element of preparation.

Study resources are also critical elements of preparation. Sometimes the resources will be a function of the preparation method selected. Other times, candidates will have to choose resources from a wide range of possibilities. A mistake in selecting resources can significantly affect test scores.

Choose a study method carefully. Because the exams measure mastery of the application of the PHR and SPHR Body of Knowledge, it is impossible to train or teach to them. Instead, knowing the HR knowledge requirements and how to apply them is the best preparation. Study methods based on the actual exams' format are preferable because they familiarize test takers with our test specifications.

The HR Certification Institute is a standard-setting and credentialing organization. As such, it does not provide professional development activities or endorse any particular study method. In fact, we strongly recommend that candidates use multiple reference materials when studying for the exams.

EXAM PREPARATION METHODS

Self-Study

Self-study can be individual, where candidates study at their own pace and on their own schedules, or it can be a group experience, where there are regular meetings, mutual assistance and lively exchanges of ideas and information among members. The key concept to self-study programs, whether individual or group-based, is flexibility.

Individual self-study requires a high degree of personal discipline. Candidates who choose this method must develop study strategies, prepare schedules and be committed to abide by those schedules. Pre-packaged preparation systems are convenient for this purpose. Any of the general HR references cited in this book can be used as a starting point for individual self-study.

A modified version of individual self-study is paired self-study. This method uses the buddy system, where two candidates pair together and use the same format as with individual self-study. It is highly flexible, yet gives candidates a support system.

Group Study

Group study offers some advantages to individual and paired self-study. The camaraderie and group support can be great assets. Many local HR association chapters sponsor certification study groups.

The following are key concepts to consider when forming a study group:

- Establish convenient meeting locations and times.
- Secure a certified HR professional to serve as a mentor to the group.
- Use pre- and post-tests using an exam similar to the one provided in the "Sample Test Questions" section of this guide.
- Design a study format with a schedule and individual member assignments.
- Use multiple resources for preparation.

When flexibility is important, self-study methods, whether individual, paired or group, are potential ways to study for the exam.

College and University Courses

Many colleges and universities offer study courses to prepare for the exams. Most often these courses are offered on a noncredit/continuing-education basis; some academic institutions, however, grant credit for these courses.

Many colleges and universities have partnered with SHRM to offer a certification preparation course using the SHRM Learning System, a study program that was developed using the HR Certification Institute's test specifications as a blueprint. Other colleges and universities use other materials.

Quality of instruction and resources should be carefully scrutinized, and it is always advisable to check references with past course participants before registering for such courses.

Chapter-Sponsored Short Courses

Many local HR association chapters offer short courses to study for the PHR and SPHR exams. These short courses provide instruction and a structured program that cover the PHR and SPHR test specifications. Contact your local SHRM chapter to determine availability of these courses in your area (for a list of SHRM chapters, visit www.shrm.org/chapters).

SHRM Certification Preparation Courses

Candidates with a good understanding of the HR field may be interested in the SHRM PHR/SPHR Certification Preparation course. This course is an intensive refresher or review of the PHR and SPHR Body of Knowledge and is designed for experienced HR practitioners who need a refresher before the exam. It is offered nationally in selected locations before each of the HR Certification Institute's exam periods.

Private Training Organizations

Some private training organizations now offer courses to prepare for the HR Certification Institute's exams. Candidates should be sure that the approach used in the course corresponds to the PHR and SPHR test specifications.

If the certification method employs instructors, it is important that they be certified. It is difficult—if not impossible—to teach about an exam one has not taken. Personal experiences of instructors offer valuable insights and increase the comfort level of examinees.

Regardless of the method, a high degree of personal commitment is needed to receive the most benefit from the preparation experience.

STRATEGIES

Any preparation method must have a strategy to maximize self-assessment and structure time, build mental and physical preparedness, and address post-exam emotions.

Self-Assessment

No two candidates bring the same education, experience and preparation to the table. As a result, it is important to conduct an honest self-assessment of your qualifications and HR work experience.

Begin by reviewing your education and work experience in light of the test specifications. Compare your resume with the test specifications. In what areas have education and experience given you a strong knowledge and application base? What will you have to work on? Make a list of your strengths and weaknesses.

Next, answer the sample test questions in this book, resisting the temptation to look at the answers before completing the test. Correct the test and total your score in each of the functional areas of the exam. Is there a correlation between the test results and the self-assessment? Keep in mind that there are only 125 sample test questions; there are 150 questions in the actual exam that count toward the final score.

The HR Certification Institute offers candidates online assessment exams at www.hrci.org/assessmentexam. These exams will help you determine your strengths and weaknesses in each of the functional areas of the exam, and allow you to become familiar with the format and difficulty level of the exam questions. There are two versions each of the PHR and SPHR assessment exams. The assessment exams are excellent indicators of preparedness for the actual exam. See page 9 for more information about the assessment exams.

These kinds of self-assessments will help candidates center on areas where the most preparation is needed. Always focus on the areas where you need the most preparation based upon the weightings of the specific exam (PHR or SPHR) you will take.

Structuring Time

Once you complete the self-assessment, map a formal approach on how you will spend your time studying for the test. Structuring time will vary depending on the level of the exam (PHR or SPHR) and the self-assessment. Sample eight-, 10- and 12-week study schedules are included on pages 33-35.

Mental and Physical Preparedness

Cramming the week or night before the exam is a common mistake many candidates make. Such behavior hurts exam performance. Preparation is best if spaced out over an extended period of time.

Given the nature of exams, a clear head will help performance more than any limited knowledge gained by last-minute cramming. The HR Certification Institute's exams are intellectually challenging and fatiguing; arriving at a test site already tired from cramming the night before is not wise. Prepare early and relax the night before the exam. Go out to eat or to a movie the night before, get a good night's rest and come to the testing center relaxed and alert.

EIGHT-WEEK SCHEDULE

PHR EXAM		SPHR EXAM	
WEEK	TOPIC	WEEK	TOPIC
1	Introduction and Pre-test	1	Introduction and Pre-test
2	Business Management and Strategy	2	Business Management and Strategy
3	Workforce Planning and Employment	3	Business Management and Strategy
4	Workforce Planning and Employment	4	Workforce Planning and Employment
5	Human Resource Development	5	Human Resource Development
6	Compensation and Benefits	6	Compensation and Benefits
7	Employee and Labor Relations	7	Employee and Labor Relations
8	Risk Management; Post-test	8	Risk Management; Post-test

Post-Exam Emotions

Upon leaving the testing center, it is common to feel frustrated because you do not know what you could have done to perform better. This emotion is common for any exam that assesses mastery in a particular field.

Unlike curriculum-based tests, these exams cannot be "taught to." Realize that these feelings of frustration are common, recognize them and be prepared to address them after the exam.

RESOURCES

Some preparation methods, such as university or college courses, will provide or identify the resources to be used in the class. Other preparation methods leave it up to the candidate. Therefore, choosing the appropriate resources is critically important.

Because the exams measure mastery of the entire PHR and SPHR Body of Knowledge, there is no single best resource to use to study for the exam.

To understand the importance of using a variety of resources, imagine a giant globe filled with marbles. Each marble represents one piece of the PHR and SPHR Body of Knowledge from each

TEN-WEEK SCHEDULE

PHR EXAM		SPHR EXAM	
WEEK	TOPIC	WEEK	TOPIC
1	Introduction and Pre-test	1	Introduction and Pre-test
2	Business Management and Strategy	2	Business Management and Strategy
3	Workforce Planning and Employment	3	Business Management and Strategy
4	Workforce Planning and Employment	4	Workforce Planning and Employment
5	Human Resource Development	5	Human Resource Development
6	Compensation and Benefits	6	Compensation and Benefits
7	Compensation and Benefits	7	Compensation and Benefits
8	Employee and Labor Relations	8	Employee and Labor Relations
9	Employee and Labor Relations	9	Employee and Labor Relations
10	Risk Management; Post-test	10	Risk Management; Post-test

of the functional areas. Each level of the exam is composed of a random drawing of marbles according to the percentage listed for each functional area in the test specifications.

If you can visualize the giant globe filled with thousands of marbles, you can easily see that it is impossible to predict which of the marbles will be on the exam. It is equally impossible for any one preparatory resource to contain all the marbles. This is why we recommend using a variety of resources for the most comprehensive exposure to the test specifications.

The HR Certification Institute's mission is to identify the applicable HR body of knowledge and to develop test specifications that measure mastery of this knowledge. It does not develop the resources to teach the test specifications to candidates. To maintain exam integrity, the HR Certification Institute separates itself from the development of preparatory resources and does not endorse any particular resource. The following, however, is a partial list of available resources. For a more complete list of resources, please refer to the resources in Section III of this guide.

TWELVE-WEEK SCHEDULE			
PHR EXAM		**SPHR EXAM**	
WEEK	TOPIC	WEEK	TOPIC
1	Introduction and Pre-test	1	Introduction and Pre-test
2	Business Management and Strategy	2	Business Management and Strategy
3	Business Management and Strategy	3	Business Management and Strategy
4	Workforce Planning and Employment	4	Workforce Planning and Employment
5	Workforce Planning and Employment	5	Workforce Planning and Employment
6	Workforce Planning and Employment Human Resource Development	6	Human Resource Development
7	Human Resource Development	7	Human Resource Development
8	Compensation and Benefits	8	Compensation and Benefits
9	Compensation and Benefits	9	Compensation and Benefits
10	Employee and Labor Relations	10	Employee and Labor Relations
11	Employee and Labor Relations	11	Employee and Labor Relations
12	Risk Management; Post-test	12	Risk Management; Post-test

There are complete learning packages that cover all functional areas of the test specifications and include self-directed modules, application activities and end-of-module exams. They are designed to follow the PHR and SPHR test specifications.

In addition, HR textbooks are a good resource. Be sure to select textbooks that are up-to-date, because the HR field changes rapidly. Textbooks published more than one or two years ago should be used with caution. It is recommended that several texts be used, rather than just one, so that candidates see different perspectives.

Custom-designed resources are used by some SHRM chapters and proprietary companies. Many of these resources are not original works. Instead, they are committee-assembled compilations of other resources.

Lending libraries are popular with some SHRM chapters. Learning resources are purchased and made available to chapter members at no cost or for a nominal fee. This allows members to review materials they may not otherwise be able to afford.

TEST-TAKING SKILLS

It is natural to have some anxiety about taking an exam; the anxiety level is likely to be even greater for candidates who have been out of school for several years.

All of the questions on the PHR and SPHR exams are multiple-choice. The question statement is called the stem and the answers are called choices. Some choices are designed to be plausible but incorrect. These are called distractors.

Questions on the exam are of different types, especially at the PHR level. Some will be identification questions, which means that definitions of concepts or facts are being assessed. Relationship questions are used to test how one concept is related to or affects another one. Other questions are application-oriented; a situation is posed and the choices reflect applying certain facts to the situation.

The following are some test-taking suggestions to help candidates perform up to their capabilities and knowledge:

- Most candidates take the exam on a computer at a testing center. There is a tutorial provided so that you can become comfortable with answering questions prior to actually beginning the exam.

- Use the white erase board that will be provided at your testing station. Feel free to make notes and simple calculations. You will be asked to return the white erase board upon completing your exam.

- Trust your first impression. There is a correct answer to each question. It is widely believed that your first impression of the correct answer will be a better choice.

- Avoid over-analyzing. Be careful not to read too much into an answer.

- Don't base your answer on your particular organization's policies or an individual experience you may have had; instead, focus on generally accepted HR practices.

- Some questions may appear to have more than one answer that is technically correct. These questions are specifically designed that way to assess your knowledge of HR by requiring you to choose the best answer. Few actual work experiences present one possible answer; indeed, HR generalists must wade through a variety of possible solutions and choose the best possible one on a daily basis. The items on the exam, then, must assess the ability to recall facts and the ability to apply them.

- If uncertain, mark the question and return to it later. If you cannot decide on an answer, mark the question and return to it after answering all of the questions on the exam. It is possible that later questions may trigger information useful for those "undecided" questions.

- Don't stop. If you are not sure how to answer a question, continue to the next one. Otherwise, you may lose valuable time. Mark the question and return to it later.

- Don't look for answer patterns. The psychometric testing process used by the HR Certification Institute ensures that questions do not fall into patterns. Contrary to some myths, "C" is not necessarily the most frequent answer and the first answer may be correct.

- The length of an answer is a false clue. It is a myth that the longer an answer, the more likely it is to be correct. It often is more difficult to write incorrect distractors than the correct answer, so it is just as likely that the longest distractor is incorrect as it is correct.

- Try to identify the answer before reading the choices. After reading the stem, try to answer the question without reading the choices. By doing this, it is more likely that one answer will stand out as being correct.

- Eliminate obvious distractors. For most questions, there are two distractors that usually appear to be incorrect, one that is likely to be plausible but incorrect, and one correct answer. When you first read a question, you should be able to eliminate two of the answers as incorrect. If you cannot decide between the other two, move on to the next question and return to the unanswered question later. (If you are taking a computer-based exam, there is a "strike-out feature" that is explained in the tutorial that will allow you to cross out the distractors you have eliminated.)

- Use "educated guesses." If you still cannot decide on a correct answer after eliminating one or two choices, choose one anyway. There is no penalty for guessing on the exam.

- Don't worry about what you don't know. If you don't know the answer to a question, don't fret about it and don't let it affect your outlook when answering other questions.

- Review your answers. After going through all of the questions on the exam, go back and answer the questions left unanswered the first time. Also, be sure that you answered all questions.

- Don't rush. There are no points for finishing early. Use the time allotted to review and check your answers. Keep in mind that someone who finishes early may know less than you do, so don't feel self-conscious about taking as much time as necessary to complete the exam. With computer-based testing, the person sitting beside you may not even be taking an HR Certification Institute exam.

SAMPLE TEST QUESTIONS

These sample questions are designed to familiarize candidates with the style and format of PHR® and SPHR® exam questions. This practice test is shorter than the actual exams (it has 125 practice items, whereas there are 150 questions on the actual exam that count toward your final score). **None of these exact questions will be found on the HR Certification Institute's exams, but they are representative of the types of questions found in them.** To help you, a scoring key and the rationale for the answers follow these practice items. The answers include how the items are coded according to the HR Certification Institute test specifications. Remember to select the best answer. Good luck!

1. "Qualified individual with a disability" refers to a person with a disability who:
   a. With reasonable accommodation can perform the essential functions of the job.
   b. Without reasonable accommodation can perform the essential functions of the job.
   c. With or without reasonable accommodation can perform the essential functions of the job.
   d. With reasonable accommodation can perform all functions of the job.

2. Which of the following positions is considered an HR specialist?
   a. Industrial relations director.
   b. Human resource manager.
   c. Personnel administrator.
   d. Human resource team leader.

3. A major concern with e-Learning is that:
   a. Retention of learned material is affected by the speed with which the learner progresses through the course.
   b. Trainees will discontinue other learning experiences critical to job performance.
   c. It is more costly than other training methodologies.
   d. It provides too much flexibility because of self-pacing.

4. What restriction is placed on NLRB certification of a unit of security guards?
   a. The same restrictions as in units of other employees.
   b. The union seeking certification must represent only guards.
   c. The expiration date of the guards' contract cannot coincide with that of the plant union.
   d. The union must include all plant employees.

5. An expatriate's expenses for home travel are deductible for U.S. tax purposes if the trip is made to:
    a. The United States.
    b. The principal residence in the United States.
    c. Anywhere outside of the country of assignment.
    d. The location of the last employment in the United States.

6. An emotional intelligence selection device is best suited for jobs requiring what characteristic?
    a. Creative application.
    b. Social interaction.
    c. Analytical thinking.
    d. Psychomotor ability.

7. Which type of data is generally unavailable to an HR manager in evaluating the effectiveness of an external employee assistance program?
    a. Initial-diagnosis category.
    b. Referral source.
    c. Utilization rate.
    d. Treatment outcome.

8. What is the most effective form of upward communication?
    a. Suggestion systems.
    b. Employee petitions.
    c. Grievance procedures.
    d. Direct discussions between supervisors and employees.

9. In which of the following content areas is it most difficult to evaluate the effectiveness of training?
    a. Typing skills.
    b. Human relations.
    c. Accident reduction.
    d. Grievance reduction.

10. Which of the following questions asked during an interview would most likely give rise to an inference of discrimination?
    a. Describe your military experience.
    b. Do you have a job-related disability?
    c. To what professional organizations do you belong?
    d. Describe the extracurricular activities you did in college.

11. In order for a union to prevail during a representation election, it must win:
    a. A majority of the votes cast in an election.
    b. Fifty-one percent of the votes of those eligible to vote in the election.
    c. Two-thirds of the votes cast in the election.
    d. Thirty percent of the votes cast.

12. When an HR department screens a large amount of information to detect emerging trends that will affect the supply of labor, it is engaging in:
    a. Intelligence.
    b. Industrial espionage.
    c. Benchmarking.
    d. Environmental scanning.

13. To ensure that a job training program is valid, a trainer will emphasize:
    a. Conducting a job/task analysis.
    b. Observing and interviewing the most productive incumbents in a job.
    c. Surveying what programs are commercially available in the specific job area.
    d. Outlining the traits necessary to perform the job.

14. Pay compression can be created by several means, including:
    a. Emphasizing external competitiveness over internal equity.
    b. Following a promotion from within a strategy.
    c. Granting increases on a percentage basis.
    d. Emphasizing job evaluation results.

15. At the beginning of a given year, a shipping department has four people, each paid $1,000 per month. In that year, each of these employees receives a pay raise of $100 per month. The raises are given Jan. 1, March 1, July 1 and Nov. 1, respectively. The salary increases raise the payroll cost for the year by:
    a. 6.25%.
    b. 7%.
    c. 9%.
    d. 10%.

16. Which of the following is true regarding how employment interviewers process applicant information?

    a. Decisions on information are made at the conclusion of the interview.

    b. Greater emphasis is placed on positive information as opposed to negative information.

    c. Pre-interview expectations do not influence the processing of information.

    d. Reasons for rejection can be specified easier than reasons for acceptance.

17. All employers with _____ or more employees must file an annual EEO-I (or I-VI) with the EEOC.

    a. 15

    b. 20

    c. 50

    d. 100

18. The most difficult problem in forecasting demand for employees is:

    a. Forecasting internal supply.

    b. Estimating turnover patterns.

    c. Determining the supply of human resources.

    d. Determining the relationship between personnel demand and the firm's output.

19. In order to prevail in a charge of discrimination based upon selecting participants for a training program, it is most appropriate for the organization to:

    a. Establish a quota system to ensure minority representation.

    b. Ensure the selection of trainees is well documented and does not have an adverse impact.

    c. Use a self-nomination method of selecting participants.

    d. Use diversity training as the initial phase of the training program.

20. Service to the customer may suffer most when which form of sales compensation is used?

    a. Salary, commission and bonus.

    b. Straight commission.

    c. Salary and commission.

    d. Bonus.

21. The biggest drawback to developing a selection program based upon a predictive validity model is:
    a. The time involved to conduct the study.
    b. Soliciting employees to participate in the study.
    c. The complexity of the statistical techniques used.
    d. The differences in job tenure of the group studied.

22. Which statement best describes organizational culture?
    a. "Our organization's value statements."
    b. "The way we do things around here."
    c. "Our company policies and procedures."
    d. "The main thing is to make sure the main thing remains the main thing."

23. In reviewing an applicant's arrest and conviction record, an employer:
    a. Can give consideration to both arrest and conviction records for specific jobs.
    b. Cannot consider conviction records.
    c. Can give consideration to arrest and conviction records.
    d. Cannot consider arrest records.

24. Which of the following may legally be stated in an organization's employee relations policy?
    a. Increase pay for remaining nonunion.
    b. Plant closure if unionized.
    c. Organizational opposition to unions.
    d. Endorsement of a specific union.

25. What is the primary purpose of a flexible benefits plan?
    a. Allow employees to contribute pre-tax dollars to buy additional benefits.
    b. Continuously update benefits options as employees' needs and desires change.
    c. Pass along benefit premium increases to employees.
    d. Combine all time-off benefits into a pool from which an employee can take time off with pay.

26. Assessment centers are used to assess:
    a. Work and interpersonal skills.
    b. Cultural fit.
    c. Technical skills.
    d. Job satisfaction.

27. Assuming no willful violation, what is the statute of limitations for recovery of back pay under the Fair Labor Standards Act?

    a. Two years.
    b. Three years.
    c. Four years.
    d. Five years.

28. During a union organization attempt, which of the following may management legally do?

    a. Promise employees a pay raise if the organizing attempt fails.
    b. Threaten to close the business if the union wins the election.
    c. Follow employees after work to determine if they visit the union hall.
    d. Hold a mandatory meeting one week before the election to explain the benefits of remaining nonunion.

29. The first step in establishing an HRIS is to:

    a. Develop the database.
    b. Determine the information needs.
    c. Establish a security and control system.
    d. Select between PC and mainframe applications.

30. An organization's primary concern is to reduce an expected labor surplus quickly. Its secondary concern is to minimize the effect on employees. The options that would best address this organization's concern by priority are:

    a. Transfers and work sharing.
    b. Layoffs and transfers.
    c. Early retirement and retraining.
    d. Natural attrition and transfers.

31. Which of the following would be a recommended compensation practice for a startup business that wishes to create an innovative, entrepreneurial culture?

    a. Offer incentive bonuses and stock ownership plans.
    b. Establish high starting pay rates to attract the most talented employees.
    c. Offer a benefits program that exceeds competitors.
    d. Establish step- or longevity-based pay increases.

32. In a matrix organizational structure:
    a. Employees have three or more supervisors.
    b. Two organizational structures exist at the same time.
    c. Productivity is enhanced because of strict functional accountability.
    d. Line authority is strengthened.

33. What is a frequent criticism of using assessment centers in organizations?
    a. Problems with establishing validity.
    b. Potential is high for adverse impact.
    c. Cost of developing and administering.
    d. Problems with the self-fulfilling prophecy.

34. A supervisor who has an employee with a suspected alcohol problem that is affecting his or her performance should:
    a. Confront the employee immediately about the alcohol problem.
    b. Diagnose the employee's problem before trying to counsel him or her.
    c. Document the situation before discussing the decreased performance with the employee.
    d. Never expect the employee to return to his or her previous performance level.

35. Which of the following criteria would be least likely to substantiate the legal defensibility of a performance appraisal system?
    a. Specific written instructions.
    b. Based on job analysis.
    c. Linked to measurable goals.
    d. Supervisors trained in administration of the system.

36. In order for a position to qualify under the executive exemption to the Fair Labor Standards Act, the position must:
    a. Be considered an officer of the organization.
    b. Require a bachelor's degree or higher.
    c. Direct the work of at least two full-time employees or the equivalent.
    d. Spend less than 30 percent of the time on nonexempt duties.

37. What kind of arbitrator is selected by the parties to serve on a single grievance case?
    a. An ad-hoc arbitrator.
    b. An interest arbitrator.
    c. A permanent umpire.
    d. A tri-partite arbitrator.

38. If a work group is highly cohesive, individuals in the group are more likely to:
    a. Be highly competitive.
    b. Value group goals.
    c. Seek status.
    d. Desire directive leadership.

39. Which type of benefits plan recognizes individual differences in terms of characteristics such as age, family status and lifestyle?
    a. Concierge.
    b. Cafeteria.
    c. Insured.
    d. Funded.

40. For virtual jobs performed by individuals shifting from project to project or working on cross-functional teams that change frequently, a job analysis must focus on the:
    a. Competencies required and how they are assessed and maintained.
    b. Knowledge, skills and abilities needed to perform the jobs.
    c. Tasks, duties and responsibilities of the virtual employees.
    d. Essential job functions needed for the changing jobs.

41. Adults learn best when the material to be taught is:
    a. Standardized.
    b. Integrated with their experience.
    c. Presented in a classroom-lecture format.
    d. Geared to the level that is slightly more difficult than they can easily handle.

42. Which of the following is an independent contractor?
    a. A temporary programmer who works part time in the data-processing department for $9 an hour.
    b. An auditor who performs a two-week audit of the company's financial records each year.
    c. A salesperson who has an office in his or her home and reports to a national sales manager.
    d. An executive who has an employment contract with a company regarding change of control.

43. A planning horizon refers to:
    a. The length of the planning cycle.
    b. The time between development and execution of a plan.
    c. The levels of strategic effect of the plan.
    d. The degree of forecasting used in the plan.

44. Which common practice in a pay-for-performance system is most likely to hinder performance?
    a. Small merit increase range amounts.
    b. Open sharing with all employees of performance expectations.
    c. A common date for merit increases.
    d. Multiple measures of employee performance.

45. When regression is used in HR research, a potential dependent variable might be:
    a. Biological data.
    b. Personal goals.
    c. Test scores.
    d. Length of employment.

46. If a candidate is recruited and hired through two professional employment agency contacts and both agencies claim the fee for the referral, what is the best approach to settling the claims?
    a. Pay the fee at 50 percent to each agency because both made the referral.
    b. Pay the full fee to each agency because both agencies referred the candidate.
    c. Recommend the two agencies negotiate the fee, because only one fee is to be paid.
    d. Examine the referral documents as to the dates referred and pay the fee to the agency whose referral was received first.

47. If the union asks the employer for use of company vehicles (when not needed for work) to transport their members to a union picnic, what is the proper response?
    a. Decline the request.
    b. Offer the use at a standard market price.
    c. Offer the use for a charge of gas and oil.
    d. Offer the use for a nominal fee.

48. A selection program must be developed for a sales representative. Place the following steps in proper sequence:

i. Identification of knowledge, skills and abilities.

ii. Job analysis.

iii. Validation as selection instrument.

iv. Development of selection instrument.

v. Identification of job-performance dimensions.

vi. Use of selection instrument.

    a. v, ii, i, iv, vi, iii.

    b. ii, i, v, iv, vi, iii.

    c. ii, v, i, iv, vi, iii.

    d. v, i, ii, iv, iii, vi.

49. What is a draw, as used for sales representatives?

    a. Money that is to be used to pay for traveling expenses.

    b. Money that is paid on a regular basis in addition to commissions.

    c. Money that is paid on a regular basis but that must be earned from commissions or paid back.

    d. Money that is paid on a regular basis to be applied against commissions but not paid back if unearned.

50. The HR control process is normally thought of as containing the following steps: I) comparing actual with expected performance; II) observing and measuring performance; III) setting expectations or standards; and IV) taking corrective action. What is the proper sequence of these steps?

    a. I, II, III, IV.

    b. II, I, IV, III.

    c. IV, II, III, I.

    d. III, II, I, IV.

51. If an HR practitioner developed an economic or statistical model to identify costs and benefits associated with an HR program, this would be called a(n):

    a. HR audit.

    b. HR accounting.

    c. Break-even analysis.

    d. Utility analysis.

52. In which training method are videotapes frequently used to illustrate how managers function in various situations?
    a. Behavior modeling.
    b. Business games.
    c. Lecture discussions.
    d. Mentoring.

53. Outplacement is the process of:
    a. Assigning a salesperson to a region outside of the home office after initial training.
    b. Placing employees in temporary positions within other companies during a period of downsizing.
    c. In-house assessment, training and placement of employees in positions in which they have previous experience.
    d. Providing a group of services to displaced employees to give assistance in employment/ career transition.

54. For many years, employees at a certain company took two daily 10-minute coffee breaks. After being organized, the company received a request for two 15-minute coffee breaks. The company should:
    a. Discontinue its practice.
    b. Continue its practice and negotiate.
    c. Discontinue its practice and negotiate.
    d. Continue the practice but refuse to negotiate.

55. Which of the following is not included in a party-in-interest as defined by ERISA?
    a. Employee with less than one year of service.
    b. Owner of at least 50 percent of the property of the employer.
    c. Trustees, custodians and persons providing services to such a plan.
    d. Administrators, fiduciaries and trustees of an employee benefits plan.

56. One problem with team-based incentives is that they:
    a. Can create competition among team members.
    b. Are more costly than individual incentives.
    c. Can result in Equal Pay Act claims.
    d. Can be perceived as unfair by high performers.

57. An organization that desires to use a job-analysis method that allows for a quick response rate and gathering of data on a large number of jobs should use which method of job analysis?
    a. Observation.
    b. Interview.
    c. Questionnaire.
    d. Functional.

58. An HR audit is a(n):
    a. Attempt to quantify the value of its human resources to the organization.
    b. Aggregate skills' inventory of the organization's human resources.
    c. Formal research effort to evaluate the current state of human resource management within the organization.
    d. Part of a human resource accounting system.

59. One well-recognized advantage of on-the-job training is:
    a. Supervisors' expertise in conducting job-specific instruction.
    b. The incorporation of unplanned activities in the learning situation.
    c. The ability to fit the learning to the trainee.
    d. The ability to expand the learning to a more developmental focus.

60. How many months after losing a representation election must a union wait before another election can be held?
    a. 6
    b. 12
    c. 24
    d. 36

61. Which of the following methods of organizational development has been criticized for the emotional stress it creates for some participants?
    a. Team building.
    b. Transactional analysis.
    c. Sensitivity training.
    d. Survey feedback.

62. For which of the following types of employees are maturity curves most used as a basis of compensation?

    a. Executives.

    b. Management trainees.

    c. Professional personnel.

    d. Long-service nonexempt employees.

63. Linking staffing levels to organizational goals is best described by which of the following?

    a. Outsourcing.

    b. Downsizing.

    c. Re-engineering.

    d. Rightsizing.

64. Employers under the OSHA Bloodborne Pathogens standard must:

    a. Provide free hepatitis B vaccinations to all employees.

    b. Establish a written exposure control plan.

    c. Communicate an employee's bloodborne infection status to co-workers upon request.

    d. Conduct regular blood tests on all employees.

65. The Worker Adjustment and Retraining Notification (WARN) Act of 1988 requires:

    a. Severance pay to workers who lose their jobs permanently.

    b. Sixty days' notice if a mass layoff or facility closing is to occur.

    c. Full disclosure regarding reasons for plant closing.

    d. A re-education allowance to workers older than 60.

66. EEOC guidelines for the Americans with Disabilities Act (ADA) specify that a particular function of a job is essential when it:

    a. Is included in the job description.

    b. Is highly specialized, requiring a high level of expertise.

    c. Requires several people to perform it.

    d. Has been performed in the past by other employees.

67. In order to reduce information overload, orientation programs should:

    a. Be modularized and spread out over a period of time.

    b. Be conducted only after an employee has served on the job for a specified period of time.

    c. Include a detailed employee reference manual for later use.

    d. Provide continuous feedback to participants.

68. The primary test to determine the reasonableness of a work rule is whether or not the:
    a. Union has requested a change in the rule or its elimination.
    b. Rule furthers a strict disciplinary approach to managing the workforce.
    c. Employees agree that the rule is necessary if the plant is to operate efficiently.
    d. Rule is reasonably related to a legitimate business reason.

69. The primary advantage of continuous recruiting is that it:
    a. Is less expensive than intermittent recruiting.
    b. Helps the employer maintain visibility and branding in the labor market.
    c. Creates the impression that the organization is growing.
    d. Results in a more efficient staffing process.

70. During negotiations, the union and company were discussing wage increases for production operators. The company claimed that granting a wage increase would give the operators more money than the supervisors were making. The union requested the salary schedules for supervisors. What is the company required to do?
    a. Refuse the request.
    b. Provide the supervisors' salary schedule to the union.
    c. Refuse the request, but give the information to a mediator.
    d. Ignore the request.

71. Which of the following is not used as a method to segment a relevant labor market?
    a. Geographic.
    b. Type of skill.
    c. Income level.
    d. Industry.

72. In training supervisors for handling discipline and discharge incidents, which of the following is the most appropriate training method?
    a. On-the-job.
    b. Case study.
    c. Programmed instruction.
    d. Role-play.

73. What is the most important requirement for a qualified benefits plan in order to be eligible for favorable tax status?

    a. The plan must integrate with Social Security.

    b. The plan must not discriminate in favor of highly compensated executives.

    c. The plan must shift income to post-working retirement years.

    d. The plan must provide some type of retirement annuity.

74. A weighted application form is most appropriate for which type of position?

    a. Top-level executive positions.

    b. Multiple incumbent positions.

    c. Positions that have underutilization of minorities.

    d. Unskilled positions.

75. An employee reports to work one morning with a weird hairstyle in order to impress the supervisor. The supervisor ignores this new hairstyle with the expectation that it will not be repeated. What type of behavior modification strategy was employed?

    a. Extinction.

    b. Punishment.

    c. Negative reinforcement.

    d. Positive reinforcement.

76. If many people perform a similar set of tasks, what would be the preferred method of collecting information for assessing training needs?

    a. Job inventory questionnaire.

    b. Employee opinion.

    c. Observation and interview.

    d. Performance appraisal data.

77. Under the duty of fair representation, a union has the responsibility to represent:

    a. Only members whose dues are current.

    b. Bargaining unit members who voted for the union.

    c. All members of the bargaining unit.

    d. All non-supervisory employees whether or not in the bargaining unit.

78. According to workers' compensation law, payment of compensation is made to an employee for any injury:
    a. Without regard to who is at fault.
    b. Only when it is due to the employer's negligence.
    c. Except for one due to the employee's carelessness.
    d. Except for one due to the negligence of a co-worker.

79. Vesting refers to:
    a. Management of retirement funds in the employee's best interest by a third party.
    b. Making funds available for pension liabilities as they occur.
    c. An employee's right to the organization's contribution to a retirement plan.
    d. The ability for employees to move retirement assets between different funds.

80. An employee reports to a manager about sexual harassment by a co-worker and asks that it "be kept quiet;" the manager then follows the employee's wishes and ignores the complaint. What is the appropriate course of action for an organization to take with regard to the situation?
    a. Inform the employee that an investigation will be conducted.
    b. Ask the employee what action should be taken.
    c. Transfer the employee to another department.
    d. Terminate the manager for not reporting the complaint.

81. In order to determine eligibility to participate in a group variable pay plan, what is the most critical question that must be answered?
    a. Can the employees influence results?
    b. How will the plan be funded?
    c. Is there low variability in performance?
    d. Who should assess the plan?

82. It is not discriminatory during pre-employment inquiries to ask about an applicant's record on:
    a. Workers' compensation.
    b. Driving.
    c. Arrests.
    d. Favoring unions.

83. A salary survey shows the following data:

ORGANIZATION	NUMBER OF INCUMBENTS	AVERAGE SALARY
A	15	$700
B	10	$700
C	25	$700
D	50	$800

How does the weighted average salary compare to the unweighted average salary?

a. It is $50 lower.

b. It is $25 lower.

c. It is $25 higher.

d. It is $50 higher.

84. An intrinsic reward is always:

a. Self-granted.

b. Monetary.

c. Esteem-based.

d. Higher order.

85. Leadership research has identified two major leader behaviors, one of which focuses on people and interpersonal relationships. What is the focus of the other?

a. Power and authority.

b. Task accomplishment.

c. Organizational culture.

d. Profitability and financial accountability.

86. When significant aspects of performance are not measured by the appraisal form, this is called:

a. Criterion contamination.

b. Criterion deficiency.

c. Rater-bias error.

d. Contrast error.

87. In a representation election conducted by the NLRB, of 230 votes cast, Union A got 40 votes, Union B got 110 votes, Union C got 80 votes and there were zero votes for "no union." Whom should the NLRB certify as the representative of the employees?
    a. Union A.
    b. Union B.
    c. Union C.
    d. A run-off election must be conducted.

88. The Uniform Guidelines on Employee Selection Procedures are:
    a. Included in amendments to the Civil Rights Act of 1991.
    b. Given great weight by the courts in considering discrimination cases.
    c. Primarily applicable to staffing decisions.
    d. Used for race discrimination cases only.

89. What is the most important factor contributing to success of a quality management program in an organization?
    a. Organizational culture supports the quality program.
    b. Union acceptance of the quality program.
    c. Statistical aptitude of supervisors in quality control.
    d. Individual rather than group awards for performance.

90. A private retirement plan must meet ERISA standards in order to:
    a. Provide a tax advantage to the employee upon retirement.
    b. Be exempted from other IRS regulations.
    c. Avoid the filing of Annual Report Form 5500.
    d. Have employer contributions count as a business expense.

91. Which management development method uses correspondence to simulate managerial decision-making?
    a. Case study.
    b. Gaming.
    c. Sensitivity groups.
    d. In-basket exercise.

92. Halo error occurs when:
    a. A large number of ratees receive ratings in the mid-range.
    b. A ratee is rated equally on multiple performance scales because of a general impression.
    c. A large number of ratees receive high ratings.
    d. No practical performance difference exists among ratees.

93. In translating the results of a salary survey into actual wage rates, what statistical technique would be most appropriate to use?
    a. Least-squares method.
    b. Dispersion method.
    c. Correlation method.
    d. Expected variance method.

94. An employment interviewer says to a job applicant, "That experience sounds interesting…," after which the interviewer pauses, waiting for the applicant to elaborate further. What type of interview technique is being used?
    a. Behavioral.
    b. Stress interview technique.
    c. Nondirective interviewing technique.
    d. Patterned interview.

95. Which of the following factors is not related to pay compression?
    a. Higher starting salaries dictated by increased market pressures.
    b. Unionized hourly pay increases that overtake supervisory and nonunion hourly rates.
    c. Merit increases that reward existing employees for higher productivity.
    d. Recruitment of new college graduates at pay levels above those of current job holders.

96. In performance appraisal systems, central tendency is the most common error found in using:
    a. Essays.
    b. Ranking.
    c. Critical incidents.
    d. Graphic rating scales.

97. Which of the following best describes the relationship between human resource planning and strategic organizational planning?
    a. Human resource planning is the essential component of strategic organizational planning.
    b. They are separate and distinct activities.
    c. Human resource planning must be completed before strategic organizational planning begins.
    d. Both types of planning are equivalent components of overall organizational planning.

98. Which is the primary advantage of using an intranet when communicating HR programs to employees?
    a. Employees are guaranteed to receive the information.
    b. Ease of keeping the information up-to-date.
    c. Increase in feedback about HR activities.
    d. Ability to keep the information internal to the organization.

99. After implementing a new job evaluation plan, it is best to deal with red circle rates by:
    a. Reducing their salary to the new maximum for their respective job grade.
    b. Allowing their base rate to increase as all others do in the same job grade.
    c. Reducing the salary to the minimum of the range and providing the employee the amount of the decrease in the form of a bonus.
    d. Freezing their salary until job-grade maximum increases to catch up with the red circle rate.

100. Race norming is a procedure whereby:
    a. Applicants are ranked on test scores, but minority group members are given bonus points.
    b. Applicants are ranked on test scores after being adjusted to the general population.
    c. Applicants are ranked on test scores within their minority group.
    d. Minority quotas are used irrespective of test scores.

101. Which of the following is most effective in improving retention?
    a. Needs analysis.
    b. Exit survey.
    c. Supervisory training.
    d. Wage analysis.

102. Testing may not be valid in predicting performance if the test measures ability but fails to measure:
    a. Education.
    b. Motivation.
    c. Talent.
    d. Skill.

103. The total span of possible work hours in a flextime environment is referred to as:
    a. Core time.
    b. Bandwidth time.
    c. Compressed work time.
    d. Contingent time.

104. Multisource assessments (360-degree appraisals) are most relevant and useful for:
    a. Retention decisions.
    b. Developmental purposes.
    c. Merit-pay decisions.
    d. Candidates for international assignments.

105. If a labor relations manager discovers that an above-average union employee who has been employed at the plant for nine years falsified an employment application by stating that he or she lost his or her previous job from layoff when, in fact, he or she was discharged, what should the manager do?
    a. Suspend the employee for 30 days.
    b. Schedule a grievance hearing as soon as possible.
    c. Discharge the employee for falsification of the application.
    d. Make the employee aware of the discovery but take no formal disciplinary action.

106. HR policies and procedures need to be fewer and less formal in organizations that exhibit a:
    a. Weak culture.
    b. Strong culture.
    c. Flat structure.
    d. Hierarchical structure.

107. A job requires a bachelor's degree in chemistry, four years of laboratory experience and the ability to use statistical computer software. These are:
    a. Position outcomes.
    b. Essential job functions.
    c. Performance standards.
    d. Job specifications.

108. A primary employer advantage of implementing a skill-based pay system is:
    a. Increased compensation costs.
    b. Increased employee productivity.
    c. Reduced training and development expenses.
    d. Ease of administration.

109. Greater flexibility for employees can be built into a vacation leave program by:
    a. Providing more vacation time.
    b. Reducing the advance notice period.
    c. Allowing a carry-over of unused leave.
    d. Having supervisors assign leave time.

110. Which type of drug test is most likely to identify individuals as drug users when, in fact, they are not?
    a. Thin-layer chromatography.
    b. Gas chromatography with mass spectrometry.
    c. Gas chromatography.
    d. Immunoassay test after an initial positive reading.

111. Which of the following common selection techniques is least predictive of workplace violence?
    a. Psychological assessments.
    b. Behavioral interviews.
    c. Reference checks.
    d. Criminal records review.

112. People are more receptive to learning in a training situation when:
    a. Management requires attendance.
    b. Peer pressure is high.
    c. E-learning is used.
    d. The material is important to them.

113. In an arbitration proceeding, it is agreed by all parties that the action complained about is a very slight departure from what is required in the labor contract. In such a case, the arbitrator is most likely to present the rule of:
    a. Reason.
    b. Parole evidence.
    c. De minimis.
    d. Management by exception.

114. The most adequate defense an employer has in a defamation-of-character lawsuit arising from providing reference information is:
    a. The absence of malice.
    b. That the information given was the truth.
    c. That the employer had a qualified privilege to provide the information.
    d. That the employee signed a release.

115. In an organization adopting a pay-for-performance philosophy:
    a. A greater amount of employee pay is "at risk."
    b. Cost-of-living increases are commonplace.
    c. Length of service is used in calculating pay increases.
    d. External competitiveness dominates compensation decisions.

116. Which of the following activities of a firm would not be part of its social responsibility?
    a. Corporate giving.
    b. Environmental protection.
    c. Civil Rights Act compliance.
    d. Diversity training.

117. For a training program designed to enhance group problem-solving skills, which type of seating management is most appropriate?
    a. Classroom style.
    b. Chevron style.
    c. Circle style.
    d. Theater style.

118. Hand tools left on an aisle floor where others may trip over them would most likely result in what level of OSHA violation?
    a. De minimis.
    b. Other than serious.
    c. Serious.
    d. Imminent danger.

119. Which of the following cannot be included in a salesperson's deductions for travel expenses for federal income tax purposes?
    a. Meal expenses.
    b. Lodging expenses.
    c. Entertainment expenses.
    d. Home-to-work commuting allowances.

120. The Civil Rights Act of 1991 provides that U.S. citizens working internationally for U.S. companies are protected by EEO laws:
    a. Except when they are in conflict with the laws of the host country.
    b. In all situations and circumstances.
    c. When they are consistent with the customs and culture of the host country.
    d. When business reasons can be established.

121. What is the main reason for the comparatively high failure rates among U.S. expatriates?
    a. Technical skill deficiency.
    b. Family and personal adjustment problems.
    c. Anti-American feelings in host countries.
    d. Polycentric thinking.

122. It is discovered by the supervisor that an employee has a part-time business that performs the same work as the organization. This has been determined to be a conflict of interest. All employees sign a conflict-of-interest policy upon hiring. Which course of action should the employee's supervisor take?
    a. Advise the employee to give up the business.
    b. Remind the employee about the policy and issue a warning.
    c. Advise the employee the part-time business activities may be continued as long as it is not done on company time.
    d. Terminate the employee immediately.

123. Tests would likely be used for evaluating the results of training programs when which criterion is used?
    a. Reaction.
    b. Learning.
    c. Behavior.
    d. Results.

124. A medical exam as part of the selection process should be:
    a. Conducted prior to making the selection decision.
    b. Scheduled after an employment offer has been extended.
    c. Eliminated as a result of the Americans with Disabilities Act.
    d. Conducted on a random basis.

125. Which of the following presents the least ethical dilemma for an HR manager to address?
    a. Specifically excluding salaries of low-paying organizations from a survey of HR positions.
    b. Referring a qualified personal friend's resume for an open position in another department.
    c. Informing employees of the reasons for the dismissal of a co-worker.
    d. Discussing an injured employee's medical condition with co-workers.

End of Sample Questions

QUICK SCORING KEY

NUMBER	ANSWER	TEST SPECIFICATION*	NUMBER	ANSWER	TEST SPECIFICATION*
1.	C	02-04	34.	C	05-06
2.	A	02-04	35.	C	03-06
3.	A	03-04	36.	C	04-01
4.	B	05-01	37.	A	05-08
5.	B	04-09	38.	B	05-04
6.	B	02-11	39.	B	04-06
7.	D	04-06	40.	A	02-05
8.	D	05-03	41.	B	03-03
9.	B	03-04	42.	B	04-01
10.	B	02-01	43.	B	01-03
11.	A	05-01	44.	A	04-02
12.	D	01-02	45.	D	02-06
13.	A	03-02	46.	D	02-08
14.	A	04-02	47.	A	05-01
15.	A	04-02	48.	C	02-11
16.	D	02-11	49.	C	04-02
17.	D	05-01	50.	D	01-06
18.	D	02-02	51.	D	01-06
19.	B	03-01	52.	A	03-03
20.	B	04-02	53.	D	02-17
21.	A	02-11	54.	B	05-11
22.	D	01-07	55.	A	04-01
23.	D	02-01	56.	D	04-02
24.	C	05-01	57.	C	02-03
25.	A	04-06	58.	C	01-06
26.	A	03-05	59.	C	03-03
27.	A	04-01	60.	B	05-01
28.	D	05-01	61.	C	01-07
29.	B	01-21	62.	C	04-02
30.	C	02-17	63.	D	02-02
31.	A	04-02	64.	B	06-01
32.	B	01-08	65.	B	05-01
33.	C	03-05	66.	B	02-01

NUMBER	ANSWER	TEST SPECIFICATION*	NUMBER	ANSWER	TEST SPECIFICATION*
67.	A	02-14	102.	B	02-11
68.	D	05-05	103.	B	05-03
69.	B	02-10	104.	B	03-07
70.	B	05-11	105.	D	05-08
71.	C	04-02	106.	B	05-05
72.	D	03-03	107.	D	02-05
73.	B	04-01	108.	B	04-02
74.	B	02-11	109.	C	04-06
75.	A	05-03	110.	D	06-05
76.	A	03-01	111.	A	06-05
77.	C	05-08	112.	D	03-03
78.	A	06-01	113.	C	05-11
79.	C	04-06	114.	B	02-01
80.	A	05-01	115.	A	04-02
81.	A	04-02	116.	C	01-05
82.	B	02-01	117.	C	03-03
83.	C	04-02	118.	B	06-01
84.	A	05-03	119.	D	04-01
85.	B	01-10	120.	A	05-01
86.	B	03-07	121.	B	02-15
87.	D	05-01	122.	A	05-05
88.	B	02-01	123.	B	03-02
89.	A	01-07	124.	B	02-01
90.	D	04-01	125.	B	01-10
91.	D	03-05			
92.	B	03-07			
93.	A	04-02			
94.	C	02-11			
95.	C	04-02			
96.	D	03-08			
97.	A	01-03			
98.	B	05-03			
99.	D	04-02			
100.	C	02-01			
101.	C	02-15			

Functional Area:

01 Business Management and Strategy

02 Workforce Planning and Employment

03 Human Resource Development

04 Compensation and Benefits

05 Employee and Labor Relations

06 Risk Management

The first two numbers refer to the specific Functional Area of the test specifications and the last two refer to the applicable Responsibility Statements in that Functional Area.

ANSWERS, RATIONALES AND CODING

1. **Answer: c. With or without reasonable accommodation can perform the essential functions of the job.** Under the Americans with Disabilities Act (ADA), a qualified individual with a disability is a person who with or without reasonable accommodation can perform the essential functions of the job. If, as a result of a job analysis, essential job functions have been identified and a person with a disability cannot perform these functions (with or without reasonable accommodation), the individual is not considered qualified. The ADA does not require employers to hire people who are not qualified even though they have a disability. Code: 02-04

2. **Answer: a. Industrial relations director.** An industrial relations director is responsible for only labor relations and safety functions. The other positions are responsible for all major HR functions. Code: 02-04

3. **Answer: a. Retention of learned material is affected by the speed with which the learner progresses through the course.** E-learning describes the use of the Internet or intranet to conduct training online. E-learning training allows employees to complete training in short periods of time with course participation and assessment tracked online. Research indicates a major problem with e-learning in long-term retention of curriculum content as a result of the speed with which the learner completes the course. Generally, e-learning is a cost-effective method that should be used in conjunction with other training methods. Code: 03-04

4. **Answer: b. The union seeking certification must represent only guards.** Due to divided loyalties and a conflict of interest, the NLRB has determined that plant guards must be in a separate union from other plant employees. During a strike situation, guards are responsible for protecting company property. Separating the guards into a different bargaining unit helps alleviate this problem. Code: 05-01

5. **Answer: b. The principal residence in the United States.** The Internal Revenue Service allows home travel expenses to be deducted from taxes, but only if the travel was to the expatriate's principal residence within the United States. Other locations are not tax deductible. Code: 04-09

6. **Answer: b. Social interaction.** Emotional intelligence is an assortment of non-cognitive skills and capabilities that influence an individual's ability to cope with environmental pressures and demands. It has five dimensions: self-management, self-awareness, self-motivation, empathy and social skills. Most studies suggest it is critical for jobs requiring a

high degree of social interaction. The other three distractors are individual in nature and are not a function of interacting with others. Code: 02-11

7. **Answer: d. Treatment outcome.** Most employee assistance programs provide periodic reports to employers outlining program activity. To protect employee confidentiality, information is compiled in such a way to guarantee anonymity. Treatment outcome is almost never reported back to the employer. The other information—initial diagnosis category, referral source and utilization—is typically found in EAP provider reports. Code: 04-06

8. **Answer: d. Direct discussions between supervisors and employees.** Personal communication between employees and supervisors is the most effective upward communication format. Research shows that competent first-line supervisors are critical for management to feel the pulse of the organization. While the other forms of upward communication may be valuable, they are less effective than personal communication between supervisors and employees. Code: 05-03

9. **Answer: b. Human relations.** All of the options except human relations can be objectively measured and quantified. Soft skills, such as human relations, can be observed but represent a challenge in terms of measurement. Code: 03-04

10. **Answer: b. Do you have a job-related disability?** Under the Americans with Disabilities Act (ADA), pre-employment inquiries about a disability are unlawful. The ADA requires a focus on essential job functions and whether the person can perform those functions with or without reasonable accommodations. Code: 02-01

11. **Answer: a. A majority of the votes cast in an election.** Much like political elections in the United States, the NLRB requires a union to win a majority of the votes during a representation election in order to certify the union. It is important, then, that all eligible employees participate in the voting to ensure that a small minority does not determine the fate of many. Code: 05-01

12. **Answer: d. Environmental scanning.** Environmental scanning is the process of studying the environment of the organization to pinpoint opportunities and threats. It involves examining government/regulatory influences, economic conditions, competitive issues and labor-force demographics. Competitive intelligence and industrial espionage examine only one of the previously mentioned areas. Benchmarking involves examining only best-in-class practices. Code: 01-02

13. **Answer: a. Conducting a job/task analysis.** A basic way to ensure the content validity of training programs is to conduct a job/task analysis. The other options are less related to content validity. Code: 03-02

14. **Answer: a. Emphasizing external competitiveness over internal equity.** Pay compression exists when pay differences between jobs of varying levels of importance become small. It is most often created by hiring practices primarily influenced by market rates. When pay progression is small, new hires earn as much as senior employees. Code: 04-02

15. **Answer: a. 6.25%.** Count up the remaining months of the increase for January (12), March (10), July (6) and November (2) (equals 30 months at $100 per month). Divide $3,000 by the total starting payroll costs ($48,000). The increase is 6.25%. Code: 04-02

16. **Answer: d. Reasons for rejection can be specified easier than reasons for acceptance.** Employment interviews can be subject to significant error from a number of different sources. Research has shown that first impressions bias the interview with decisions made in the first few minutes. Also, negative information has greater effect than positive information. As a result, interviewers can articulate reasons for applicant rejection far more easily than reasons for applicant acceptance. Code: 02-11

17. **Answer: d. 100.** The EEOC requires all employers with 100 or more employees to annually file an EEO-I report. The report numbers vary by type of organization:
    EEO-1 Private Business
    EEO-2 Joint Apprenticeship Committees
    EEO-3 Unilateral Apprenticeship Programs
    EEO-4 State and Local Governments
    EEO-5 Public Elementary and Secondary Schools
    EEO-6 Colleges and Universities
    Code: 05-01

18. **Answer: d. Determining the relationship between personnel demand and the firm's output.** The demand for human resources is often directly related to the expected demand for the firm's products and/or services. In addition, the organization's objectives and productivity are important determinants. Code: 02-02

19. **Answer: b. Ensure the selection of trainees is well documented and does not have an adverse impact.** Training is a condition of employment subject to EEO laws. As such, participation opportunities come under the Uniform Guidelines on Employee Selection Procedures (especially when training opens up promotional opportunities). Adverse impact calculations should be made on selection of trainees using the 4/5's rule. Code: 03-01

20. **Answer: b. Straight commission.** When sales representatives are paid commission only, there is a tendency to emphasize sales at the expense of service after the sale. When service after the sale is important, organizations generally include salary as part of the compensation package to reward employees for time spent in providing customer service. Code: 04-02

21. **Answer: a. The time involved to conduct the study.** Predictive validity measures test results compared with subsequent job performance. It is an "after-the-fact" measure. The EEOC prefers predictive validity because it is most closely tied to job performance. It usually requires a large sample of employees (greater than 30) and time gap (usually one year) between the test and performance. The time gap generally presents the biggest obstacle to employers. Code: 02-11

22. **Answer: d. "The main thing is to make sure the main thing remains the main thing."** Behaviors are the best indicators of organizational culture. The way things are done is the best indicator of the values and beliefs of an organization. Formal written value statements and policies and procedures are not always indicative of the true beliefs of an organization. "The main thing is to make sure the main thing remains the main thing" is the key determinant of how a strategy is executed. Code: 01-07

23. **Answer: d. Cannot consider arrest records.** Arrest records have been consistently found by courts to result in disparate impact on some racial and minority groups protected by the Civil Rights Act. Arrest records do not indicate guilt. Employers may use conviction records, especially if the offense was job-related. Even conviction records do not serve as an absolute bar to employment. They must be viewed in relation to the nature of the offense and time period in which it occurred. Code: 02-01

24. **Answer: c. Organizational opposition to unions.** An organization can legally state opposition to the unionization of employees. A pay increase for remaining nonunion is a promise that constitutes an unfair labor practice. Likewise, a plant closure is a threat and also an unfair labor practice if done only to avoid the union. Endorsement of a specific union is also an unfair labor practice that could be construed as setting up a "company union."
Code: 05-01

25. **Answer: a. Allow employees to contribute pre-tax dollars to buy additional benefits.** The primary benefit of a flexible benefits plan involves favorable tax treatment under the Internal Revenue Code. Employees are able to use pre-tax dollars to purchase additional benefits. Code: 04-06

26. **Answer: a. Work and interpersonal skills.** An assessment center is a collection of individual and group instruments and exercises designed to assess a person for a job or to identify a person's developmental needs. Assessment-center exercises almost exclusively measure managerial and interpersonal skills. Code: 03-05

27. **Answer: a. Two years.** The FLSA has a two-year statute of limitation for recovery of back pay. In cases of a willful or intentional violation, a three-year statute of limitation is available. Records should be kept for this three-year period unless state law requires a more stringent standard. Code: 04-01

28. **Answer: d. Hold a mandatory meeting one week before the election to explain the benefits of remaining nonunion.** The National Labor Relations Act (Wagner Act) identifies certain unfair labor practices on the part of employers. Employers cannot interfere with employees' rights to organize. Interference means that an employer cannot threaten, promise, coerce, interrogate or spy on employees exercising their legally protected rights. The Labor Management Relations Act (Taft-Hartley Act) permits "captive audience" speeches. In Peerless v. Plywood Co., employers are prohibited from making speeches to mass assemblies of employees within 24 hours before an election is scheduled to be held. Code: 05-01

29. **Answer: b. Determine the information needs.** An HRIS supports organizational decision-making; therefore, the first step is to determine the specific information needs. The other options, while important, should follow the analysis of information needs. Code: 01-21

30. **Answer: c. Early retirement and retraining.** Early retirement and retraining would result in the quickest reduction in head count with the least disruption to employees. Natural attrition is dependent on employee timing. Layoffs, transfers and work sharing would most likely result in negative reactions from employees. With early retirement and retraining, the employer is in a better position to influence departures without negative consequences. Code: 02-17

31. **Answer: a. Offer incentive bonuses and stock ownership plans.** Incentive bonuses and stock plans focus employee behavior on building the company. They allow employees to share in the success of the company. High fixed-cost compensation programs are not appropriate for startup organizations. Code: 04-02

32. **Answer: b. Two organizational structures exist at the same time.** With a matrix organizational structure, two organizational structures exist at the same time—

a conventional-functional organization and a project-team organization. Employees join a project team but retain their positions in the conventional-functional organization. Matrix structures are often prevalent in new product development. Code: 01-08

33. **Answer: c. Cost of developing and administering.** Assessment centers are a collection of instruments and exercises designed to provide a standardized evaluation of behavior on multiple inputs. The evaluation can be used for selection and development purposes. The instruments and exercises can include background interviews, performance tests, in-baskets, leaderless group discussions and case analysis. Assessment centers tend to be extremely objective, valid and less subject to adverse impact. They, however, are costly to develop. Much time and cost is put into creating the exercises, training assessors and administering the assessment center. Code: 03-05

34. **Answer: c. Document the situation before discussing the decreased performance with the employee.** In general, supervisors are ill-equipped to handle alcohol-related problems in the workplace. They should not confront or counsel someone suffering from alcoholism, but they should address the situation as a performance problem and refer the employee to professional help. Code: 05-06

35. **Answer: c. Linked to measurable goals.** To be legally defensible, performance appraisals should be based upon a job analysis to establish the job-relatedness. Specific written instructions and training should be provided to supervisors in order to standardize the process to minimize adverse impact. Even though performance appraisal criteria may be linked to measurable goals, there is no way of determining whether those goals are relevant to the job and are being consistently measured. Code: 03-06

36. **Answer: c. Direct the work of at least two full-time employees or the equivalent.** Under the FLSA, an executive must have primary duties managing the enterprise (or a division); customarily and regularly direct the work of at least two full-time employees or the equivalent; be compensated on a salary basis at a rate not less than $455 per week; and have the authority to hire or fire other employees, or the employee's recommendations as to change of status of other employees must be given particular weight. Code: 04-01

37. **Answer: a. An ad-hoc arbitrator.** An ad-hoc arbitrator sits on a per-case basis. An interest arbitrator is used in collective bargaining. A permanent umpire serves as an arbitrator for the life of the labor contract. A tri-partite arbitrator is really an arbitration panel of three persons that may be ad hoc or permanent in nature. Code: 05-08

38. **Answer: b. Value group goals.** Cohesive work groups place a large emphasis on group goals. They are seldom internally competitive, and group outcomes supersede individual attention (status). Code: 05-04

39. **Answer: b. Cafeteria.** In cafeteria plans, each employee is allotted an amount of money for benefits, usually after deductions for minimum benefit coverage and legally required benefits. The employee can then elect additional benefits based upon his or her personal circumstances. The employee, in essence, is able to tailor benefits to his or her situation. Code: 04-06

40. **Answer: a. Competencies required and how they are assessed and maintained.** Because of the changing nature of virtual jobs, the traditional emphasis on knowledge, skills, abilities and essential job functions is not flexible enough to meet the requirements of the virtual workplace where multifaceted competencies determine success. Code: 02-05

41. **Answer: b. Integrated with their experience.** Adult learning differs from other forms of learning in that trainee experience can be integrated into the learning process to make the learning process more meaningful. Traditional learning models such as classroom lecture and programmed instruction do not allow the flexibility of experiential development. Code: 03-03

42. **Answer: b. An auditor who performs a two-week audit of the company's financial records each year.** The Internal Revenue Service has established an 11-factor test in making an independent-contractor determination. (This is a streamlined version of the 20-factor test in use since 1987.) Primary factors include: Does the individual own his or her own facilities or equipment? Is there an opportunity to make a profit or loss? Are the services available to others? How much supervision is exercised? Code: 04-01

43. **Answer: b. The time between development and execution of a plan.** The time between development and execution of a plan is the planning horizon. Horizons can generally differ in length from short-term (one year), intermediate-term (one to three years) or long-term (three to 10 years). HR needs to develop plans that address all three horizons in order to be truly strategic. Code: 01-03

44. **Answer: a. Small merit increase range amounts.** Small pay increase ranges can significantly hinder performance. Typically, a merit increase range needs to be above 8% to significantly affect employee performance. Code: 04-02

45. **Answer: d. Length of employment.** The purpose of regression analysis is to use the correlation between two or more variables to determine how one can be predicted from the others. Biographical data, personal goals and test scores are independent variables. Length of employment and performance data are considered to be dependent variables. Code: 02-06

46. **Answer: d. Examine the referral documents as to the dates referred and pay the fee to the agency whose referral was received first.** Although the other options all seem plausible, the HR manager is faced with an issue of contract law. The rule of thumb is that the first to refer receives the fee. Most agency contracts contain language to that effect. Code: 02-08

47. **Answer: a. Decline the request.** Under Section 8 of the National Labor Relations Act (Wagner Act), it is an unfair labor practice for an employer to dominate or interfere with the information or administration of any labor organization, or to contribute financial or other support to it. The use of company vehicles would be viewed as supporting the union. Code: 05-01

48. **Answer: c. ii, v, i, iv, vi, iii.** In developing a selection program, an employer begins by conducting a job analysis of the position in question. The next step is to determine job-performance dimensions or how success is defined for the job. Next, worker characteristics such as knowledge, skills, abilities and other characteristics are identified. Development of assessment devices (selection instrument) to measure those characteristics takes place. The selection instrument is then used and validated. Code: 02-11

49. **Answer: c. Money that is paid on a regular basis but that must be earned from commissions or paid back.** A draw is an amount advanced and repaid from future commissions. A draw system allows salespersons to even out compensation between high and low sales periods. A risk to employers is that future commission may not be large enough to cover the draw. Code: 04-02

50. **Answer: d. III, II, I, IV.** Much like setting the temperature on a thermostat, the HR control process involves setting expectations/standards, observing/measuring performance, comparing actual to expected performance and taking corrective action if necessary. Code: 01-06

51. **Answer: d. Utility analysis.** A utility analysis builds an economic or statistical model to identify the costs and benefits associated with specific HR programs or activities. Utility analysis is one of the basic ways to establish the worth of HR programs. Code: 01-06

52. **Answer: a. Behavior modeling.** In behavior modeling, trainees observe a supervisor role-play in a common work situation. Because situations presented are typical of those encountered, trainees are able to relate it to their own jobs. Code: 03-03

53. **Answer: d. Providing a group of services to displaced employees to give assistance in employment/career transition.** Outplacement or career-transition services are often provided when employees are displaced through elimination of jobs or because of performance. Services typically include personal career counseling, resume preparation, interviewing training, referral assistance and support services. Code: 02-17

54. **Answer: b. Continue its practice and negotiate.** Coffee breaks are a mandatory subject for negotiation. However, the employer is under no obligation to change past practice until the item has been negotiated. Unions often attempt to change past practice outside of the bargaining environment. The employer's best strategy is to deal with the issue through the formalized structure of collective bargaining. Code: 05-11

55. **Answer: a. Employee with less than one year of service.** Under ERISA, a party-in-interest includes all individuals who come under or have impact on a qualified plan. Owners, trustees, administrators, etc., are all considered a party-in-interest. Until an individual becomes a plan participant, he or she is not considered a party-in-interest. Code: 04-01

56. **Answer: d. Can be perceived as unfair by high performers.** Team-based incentives are allocated on an equal basis whereby each team member gets a pro rata share of the total award based upon team performance. This system can result in perceptions by high performers that they are not being recognized for their performance. In addition, it can allow marginal performers to share equally in the award. Code: 04-02

57. **Answer: c. Questionnaire.** Questionnaires, as a means of gathering job-analysis data, provide the most efficient use of resources when data must be collected on many jobs. Questionnaires are self-administered, allowing them to be given to many participants at once. They may be open-ended to allow greater flexibility, or highly structured to fit compensation or validation needs. Observation is very time-consuming, especially for long-cycle jobs. Likewise, individual interviews require quite a bit of time. Functional job analysis, used by the federal government, is highly structured and requires extensive resources. Code: 02-03

58. **Answer: c. Formal research effort to evaluate the current state of human resource management within the organization.** An HR audit is a systematic study of the HR functions performed—or not performed—in the organization. It identifies strengths, weaknesses and corrective action. Code: 01-06

59. **Answer: c. The ability to fit the learning to the trainee.** On-the-job training is a planned skills training conducted by supervisors or experienced co-workers. Unfortunately, many supervisors and co-workers are not trained on how to give specific job-related feedback necessary for training transfer. Its primary advantage is that it can be tailored to the individual employee. It is one of the most cost-effective training methods. Code: 03-03

60. **Answer: b. 12.** Whether the union wins or loses, a representation election cannot be held involving the same bargaining unit of employees for at least 12 months. As a result, union activity tends to drop off. Code: 05-01

61. **Answer: c. Sensitivity training.** Organizational development (OD) is designed to increase an organization's effectiveness through planned interventions using behavioral-science knowledge. A number of techniques are used in OD, including sensitivity training. This method makes individuals aware of themselves and the effect they have on others. Sensitivity training features an unstructured group with no specific agenda. The interaction that takes place in these groups is apparently quite threatening to some people. Code: 01-07

62. **Answer: c. Professional personnel.** Maturity curves are a compensation plan that depicts the relationship between experience in a career field and pay level. They are most appropriate to professionals in science, engineering, architecture and related fields. Code: 04-02

63. **Answer: d. Rightsizing.** Rightsizing is a broader concept than downsizing or outsourcing. It can include expanding the workforce. The common theme of rightsizing is efficient use of human talent. Downsizing is an activity designed to create more efficient operation through layoffs. Outsourcing is the use of outside firms to provide necessary products and services. Re-engineering is the process of starting with customer needs, recreating an organization structure to meet those needs, and considering internal and external human resources to fit the new structure. Code: 02-02

64. **Answer: b. Establish a written exposure control plan.** The OSHA Bloodborne Pathogens standard requires employers subject to OSHA that have any employees with on-the-job exposure to blood or other bodily fluids to take the following steps:
    1. Establish a written exposure-control plan.
    2. Observe universal precautions.
    3. Identify and adopt engineering and work-practice controls.
    4. Provide personal protective equipment.
    5. Develop housekeeping, waste management and laundry standards.
    6. Make available free hepatitis B vaccinations to those employees with occupational exposure.

7. Establish post-exposure evaluation.

8. Communicate hazards to employees.

9. Maintain specific record keeping.

Code: 06-01

65. **Answer: b. Sixty days' notice if a mass layoff or facility closing is to occur.** The WARN Act was intended to provide affected workers, their union (if present), elected public officials and state employment services advance notice of impending mass layoffs and/or plant closings. Nothing in the WARN Act requires severance pay, re-education or retraining allowances, or disclosure of the circumstances regarding the layoff or closing. Code: 05-01

66. **Answer: b. Is highly specialized, requiring a high level of expertise.** "Essential job functions refers to the fundamental duties of an employment position the individual with a disability holds or desires. The term essential job function does not include marginal functions of the position" (42 U.S.C. 12116 part 1630). Several reasons for considering a function essential include the reason the position exists is to perform the function, because limited employees perform the function, or it is highly specialized so the incumbent in the position is hired for his or her expertise or ability to perform the function. Code: 02-01

67. **Answer: a. Be modularized and spread out over a period of time.** Too much information given too fast creates information overload and reduces information retention. To minimize this problem, orientation activities should be divided into manageable units and spread out over time. Code: 02-14

68. **Answer: d. Rule is reasonably related to a legitimate business reason.** Work rules cannot be arbitrary and capricious. They must relate to a legitimate business reason in order to be upheld. Code: 05-05

69. **Answer: b. Helps the employer maintain visibility and branding in the labor market.** Recruiting is not a process that can be turned off and on. A continuous recruiting process, although more costly, keeps the employer visible in the labor market. When recruiting without open positions, the employer must carefully manage the process so that applicants don't feel they have wasted their time, which will result in negative public perception. Code: 02-10

70. **Answer: b. Provide the supervisors' salary schedule to the union.** Management has a duty to provide relevant information to a union for collective bargaining purposes. Determining what is relevant is often problematic. If a rationale for not granting a pay

increase involves a pay-compression problem with supervisors, the union is entitled to such information. If management did not use this rationale, it would be under no obligation to provide the supervisors' salary schedule. Code: 05-11

71. **Answer: c. Income level.** For compensation purposes, a relevant labor market is defined as the market from which an organization secures new employees or to which it loses current employees. Income level is not a traditional labor market for survey purposes, whereas geographic, skill and industry represent relevant defined labor markets. Code: 04-02

72. **Answer: d. Role-play.** Role-play requires the trainee to assume a role in a mock situation and act out that role. It is behavioral-based and allows for feedback on the trainee's performance. Discipline and discharge training is ideally suited for role-playing. Code: 03-03

73. **Answer: b. The plan must not discriminate in favor of highly compensated executives.** The Internal Revenue Service has stated that for a benefits plan to qualify for tax-favored status, it must be a definite written plan and arrangement that is communicated to the employees and established and maintained by an employer for the exclusive benefit of employees or beneficiaries. As such, the plan cannot discriminate in favor of certain highly compensated employees. Code: 04-01

74. **Answer: b. Multiple incumbent positions.** Weighted applications are designed using job analysis and performance appraisal data. Certain responses are given weights or numerical scores based on performance data. Weighted applications are time-consuming and must be periodically validated. Because of this, they are most appropriate for multiple incumbent positions. Code: 02-11

75. **Answer: a. Extinction.** Extinction is ignoring behavior. Punishment includes sending the employee home until the hairstyle is changed. Negative reinforcement exists if the supervisor criticizes the hairstyle. Positive reinforcement involves the supervisor complimenting the employee on the hairstyle. Code: 05-03

76. **Answer: a. Job inventory questionnaire.** Job inventory questionnaires can be administered to a large group of employees in a short amount of time to identify training needs. The other identified methods are more time-consuming. Code: 03-01

77. **Answer: c. All members of the bargaining unit.** The Labor Management Relations Act requires unions to represent all employees covered by the collective bargaining agreement, whether or not they are union members. Employees can bring civil action against a union that breaches this duty (29 U.S.C. & 159). Unions need to judge whether a grievance has

merit and typically will err on the conservative side. This often results in overburdening the grievance system, costing both parties time and money. Code: 05-08

78. **Answer: a. Without regard to who is at fault.** Workers' compensation is designed to provide no-fault coverage for work-related injuries and illnesses. The passage of workers' comp statutes took away from employees the right to raise defenses of contributory negligence on the employee or co-worker's part and on the employer's part. Code: 06-01

79. **Answer: c. An employee's right to the organization's contribution to a retirement plan.** Vesting is an earned interest into employer contributions to a retirement plan. Once earned, the employee has a legal right to those contributions/funds. Code: 04-06

80. **Answer: a. Inform the employee that an investigation will be conducted.** Once a manager has constructive knowledge of sexual harassment, the organization can be held liable. Even though the employee wishes to keep the allegation confidential, with no action by the organization, there is an affirmative duty to investigate and act on the results of the investigation. The manager may be subject to discipline; however, an investigation is a must. Code: 05-01

81. **Answer: a. Can the employees influence results?** There are three types of true group variable pay programs: group sharing, goal sharing and profit sharing. Each must be predetermined and have the ability of employees to influence results. The other three questions are all issues that can be addressed in plan design. Code: 04-02

82. **Answer: b. Driving.** Asking about a driving record is legitimate if the future employee has to drive as part of his or her duties. Inquiries about workers' compensation may be illegal under the ADA. Inquiries about arrest records have a disproportionate effect on minority group members. Employers may not discriminate based upon union preference. Code: 02-01

83. **Answer: c. It is $25 higher.** The unweighted average salary is 700 + 700 + 700 + 800 (2,900) divided by 4 = $725.

   The weighted average salary is calculated as follows:
   15 x 700 = 10,500
   10 x 700 = 7,000
   25 x 700 = 17,500
   50 x 800 = 40,000
   75,000 divided by 100 = $750
   Code: 04-02

84. **Answer: a. Self-granted.** There are two large categories of motivation: extrinsic and intrinsic. Extrinsic motivation assumes people are motivated by external factors such as pay, recognition, praise, etc. Intrinsic motivation assumes people are motivated from within by internal factors such as interesting work, curiosity, pride, etc. Code: 05-03

85. **Answer: b. Task accomplishment.** This item comes from leadership research from Ohio State that identified two leader behaviors of consideration and initiating structure; University of Michigan researchers who identified production-centered and employee-centered leadership; and the Blake and Mouton Managerial Grid, which uses as its dimensions concerns for the task and concern for people. Code: 01-10

86. **Answer: b. Criterion deficiency.** Criterion deficiency occurs when significant aspects of job performance are not captured by the appraisal instrument. Criterion contamination occurs when the appraisal instrument captures factors irrelevant to performance. Rater bias is the prejudice of the rater that influences ratings. Contrast error is rating one employee higher or lower, not because of objective performance but because of how he or she compares to another employee. Code: 03-07

87. **Answer: d. A run-off election must be conducted.** To prevail in a union election, one party must receive a majority of the votes cast. In this case, 230 votes were cast. Because no party received greater than 115 votes, the NLRB would order a run-off election as required by the Taft-Hartley Act. Code: 05-01

88. **Answer: b. Given great weight by the courts in considering discrimination cases.** The Uniform Guidelines on Employee Selection Procedures represent a joint statement of the EEOC, the Civil Service Commission, the Department of Labor and the Department of Justice on acceptable selection procedures. These guidelines are not legally binding but represent sound scientific practice and serve as a primary reference point for courts. Judges give great deference to these guidelines. They apply to more than selection instruments, namely job performance measures and record keeping. Code: 02-01

89. **Answer: a. Organizational culture supports the quality program.** Research shows the number one determinant of success in a total quality management (TQM) program is support by all members of the organization. TQM is not a single technique, but a total philosophy for operating an organization. Although union acceptance of the TQM program and statistical aptitude of supervisors are factors that can affect success, they are far less important than organizational support. Code: 01-07

90. **Answer: d. Have employer contributions count as a business expense.** Under ERISA, a retirement plan may treat employer contributions as an expense for accounting purposes, which allows an organization to use retirement contributions to offset current year taxes. Distributions from ERISA-qualified retirement plans are subject to federal income tax withholding and other IRS regulations. ERISA-qualified plans must file a Form 5500 depending on the number of participants covered. Code: 04-01

91. **Answer: d. In-basket exercise.** In-basket exercises are frequently used in management-development programs. "Incoming mail" is given to trainees who must decide what, if any, action is to be taken. These exercises focus on problem-solving and decision-making skills. Code: 03-05

92. **Answer: b. A ratee is rated equally on multiple performance scales because of a general impression.** Halo effect or error occurs when one allows a prominent characteristic to overshadow other evidence. One aspect of performance contaminates other aspects of performance in a positive manner. The reverse effect is referred to as "horned" effect, when the performance is viewed in a negative manner. The other options are potential problems with performance appraisal ratings in general. Code: 03-07

93. **Answer: a. Least-squares method.** The least-squares method of regression analysis is a technique for fitting a line to data plotted on a graph to determine the degree of correlation (or significance) between two variables. In building a salary structure, the plotted line is referred to as the "trend line" and salary grades are based on it. Code: 04-02

94. **Answer: c. Nondirective interviewing technique.** A nondirective interview uses general open-ended questions from which other probing questions can be asked. Nondirective interviews are less threatening to the interviewee and allow a broader discussion. A potential difficulty associated with nondirective interviews involves obtaining standardized information from interviewees. Code: 02-11

95. **Answer: c. Merit increases that reward existing employees for higher productivity.** Pay compression exists when pay differentials between new hires and long-term employees are small or when pay differentials between supervisors and those supervised are small. Merit increases very seldom cause pay compression. Code: 04-02

96. **Answer: d. Graphic rating scales.** Central tendency is a common problem associated with a performance appraisal that uses a graphic rating scale. The rater evaluates all employees as average or in the mid-range of the scale. In effect, the rater is not making any judgments. Code: 03-08

97. **Answer: a. Human resource planning is the essential component of strategic organizational planning.** Human resource planning must flow from and complement strategic organizational planning. Strategic planning involves identifying organizational objectives and actions needed to achieve those objectives. Human resource planning involves analyzing the need for and availability (or unavailability) of human resources so that the organization can meet its objectives. Code: 01-03

98. **Answer: b. Ease of keeping the information up-to-date.** One of the intranet's primary advantages as a communication medium is its ability to provide current and timely information. There are no guarantees that employees receive the information. Opening an e-mail legally does not signify receipt. Feedback could actually decrease or increase as the result of the intranet. Although intranets are supposed to be secure, employees may print HR information and share it externally. Code: 05-03

99. **Answer: d. Freezing their salary until job-grade maximum increases to catch up with the red circle rate.** A red circle rate is where the incumbent is paid above the rate-range maximum for the job. Red circle rates come about either through the administration of a new job evaluation plan or when an employee takes a demotion. The standard practice for handling red circle rates is to freeze the incumbent's salary until the range catches up to the rate. Code: 04-02

100. **Answer: c. Applicants are ranked on test scores within their minority group.** Race norming involves the adjustment of employment test scores or use of alternative score mechanisms based on race or gender. The Civil Rights Act of 1991 prohibited race norming. With race norming, test scores are ranked for minority and majority groups. Separate cut-off scores are usually established for each group. Code: 02-01

101. **Answer: c. Supervisory training.** Research has consistently shown that the relationship that an employee has with his or her supervisor is the single greatest factor affecting his or her decision to leave a company. Therefore, of the choices listed, supervisory training has the greatest potential to reduce turnover and improve employee retention. Code: 02-15

102. **Answer: b. Motivation.** Industrial psychologists believe that the best indication of future performance is past performance. Performance is a function of skills and abilities multiplied by motivation. Skills and abilities determine whether someone "can do" a job. Motivation determines whether someone "will do" a job. Both must be measured to have a valid selection outcome. Code: 02-11

103. **Answer: b. Bandwidth time.** Bandwidth time refers to the total range of hours when employees can begin and end work. Core time refers to those hours when all employees must be at work. If an employee must work eight hours between 6:00 a.m. and 6:00 p.m., the time between 6:00 a.m. and 6:00 p.m. is referred to as bandwidth time. Code: 05-03

104. **Answer: b. Developmental purposes.** Multisource assessments are referred to as 360-degree feedback, full-circle feedback and multi-rater assessment. First, critical competencies, behaviors or values are identified. Then managers are evaluated on these skill sets by having direct reports, internal and external customers, peers or co-workers, or superiors complete a confidential survey about the person's ability. The summarized data are shared with the manager for developmental purposes. Multisource assessments are popular in team environments. Code: 03-07

105. **Answer: d. Make the employee aware of the discovery but take no formal disciplinary action.** In this situation, the falsification occurred so long ago that it is highly unlikely an arbitration would uphold a grievance or termination. A "stale" past record serves to set aside any disciplinary action, especially given a good current performance record. Code: 05-08

106. **Answer: b. Strong culture.** Strong cultures are self-managing. They rely on consistency through the culture itself without extensive controls. The structure of the organization has little effect on the degree of formalization of the policies and procedures. Code: 05-05

107. **Answer: d. Job specifications.** A specification is the skills, knowledge and abilities that an individual needs to perform a job satisfactorily. Job specifications can include education, experience, work skill requirements, personal abilities, and mental and physical requirements. Essential job functions are the fundamental duties of a position. Position outcomes and performance standards are performance-related criteria for a position. Code: 02-05

108. **Answer: b. Increased employee productivity.** The primary employer advantage is increased productivity from a higher-skilled workforce. In addition, a skills-based pay system provides increased compensation to employees as they master and become certified in new skills. These systems are person-based, as opposed to job-based. They pay for skill mastery as opposed to responsibility. These plans provide job enrichment and job security for employees. They allow for the opportunity to earn more pay. In practice, payroll costs are less because of increased workforce flexibility and decreased staffing. Code: 04-02

109. **Answer: c. Allowing a carry-over of unused leave.** Accrual of vacation leave along with year-end carry-over allows employees to accumulate vacation leave for special occasions. If the amount of carry-over is great, it can create a cash flow problem for employers when taken or paid out upon termination. Code: 04-06

110. **Answer: d. Immunoassay test after an initial positive reading.** The most common form of drug testing is the immunoassay test. It has high sensitivity to detect small amounts of drugs and cross reactivity to detect small amounts of similar drugs that may not be illegal. Consequently, it results in large numbers of false positives. The other three options are all confirmatory tests used in conjunction with an immunoassay test after an initial positive reading. These options are generally more precise in identifying illegal drugs above a minimum threshold. Code: 06-05

111. **Answer: a. Psychological assessments.** Given what is known about violent behavior in the workplace, no psychological tests can adequately assess an employee's circumstances, feelings and thoughts to make an accurate prediction of how that person will behave. Well-designed job-related behavioral interview questions can predict violence potential when they assess past human relations skills, coping skills (i.e., stress tolerance) and organizational fit. Likewise, both reference checks and criminal records review are based upon the adage that the best indicator of future performance is past performance. Behavior has a strong tendency to repeat itself. Code: 06-05

112. **Answer: d. The material is important to them.** Research on adult learning shows that training is best received when there is a relationship between training and important job outcomes. Receptivity is higher when relevance is high. Code: 03-03

113. **Answer: c. De minimis.** Minor violations of a collective bargaining agreement are generally not accorded much weight by arbitrators. These "de minimis" violations, while technically wrong, do not generally result in substantial harm to either party. Only when a pattern of such "de minimis" violations is demonstrated will an arbitrator remedy in an award. Code: 05-11

114. **Answer: b. That the information given was the truth.** The ultimate or absolute defense in a defamation-of-character lawsuit is the truth. For a plaintiff to prevail, he or she must show that the information provided was a lie. Although the other options to this item are defenses, the truth provides the most protection for the employer. Code: 02-01

115. **Answer: a. A greater amount of employee pay is "at risk."** Pay-for-performance systems are becoming very popular because of their perceived relationship to organizational

performance. In a pay-for-performance system, no increases are given except when justified by objective measurable performance increases. Code: 04-02

116. **Answer: c. Civil Rights Act compliance.** Social responsibility is the idea that business has social obligations above and beyond making a profit. It goes beyond complying with the law—in this case, the Civil Rights Act. Voluntary actions establish a positive company reputation and brand. Code: 01-05

117. **Answer: c. Circle style.** Circle and horseshoe seating arrangements are especially suited for highly interactive training such as group problem solving. Classroom, chevron and theater seating lend themselves to large group presentations with less trainer-participant interaction. Code: 03-03

118. **Answer: b. Other than serious.** Other-than-serious violations could have an effect on an employee's health and safety but probably would not cause death or serious harm. A "de minimis" violation is a condition that is not directly and immediately related to an employee's health and safety. A serious violation is one where the condition could probably cause death and serious harm and the employee should know of the danger. An imminent-danger violation is one where there is reasonable certainty that the condition will cause death or serious harm if not corrected immediately. Code: 06-01

119. **Answer: d. Home-to-work commuting allowances.** The first three options are legitimate sales-related expenses that qualify under the Internal Revenue Codes as deductible expenses. Home-to-work travel is not a sales-related expense. Code: 04-01

120. **Answer: a. Except when they are in conflict with the laws of the host country.** The Civil Rights Act of 1991 extended coverage of U.S. EEO laws to U.S. citizens working abroad, except where local laws or customs conflict. Code: 05-01

121. **Answer: b. Family and personal adjustment problems.** Family and personal adjustment problems are the single largest cause of failure of expatriates. These problems can be addressed through proper selection of expatriates (and their families), in-depth training on resolving these problems, and organizational systems to support the expatriation process. Code: 02-15

122. **Answer: a. Advise the employee to give up the business.** Work rules and procedures need to be consistently enforced. The employee should be advised to give up the business. A conflict-of-interest policy should not be waived, especially when all employees are expected to comply. If the employee refuses to give up the business, then termination of employment is appropriate. Code: 05-05

123. **Answer: b. Learning.** Trainee reaction to the value of training programs is probably the most frequent criterion used to evaluate training programs. In this approach, trainees are asked (often using questionnaires) whether the training is useful. Learning is what trainees can demonstrate that they know as a result of the training. Using tests, it can be determined if they have learned successfully. When behavior is the criterion, the focus is on whether the learning will be applied on the job. Behaviors are most likely to be measured through a performance appraisal system such as BARS. Trainees may believe the training to be useful (reaction); they may even use newly acquired techniques on the job (behavior). However, organizations should be interested in results. Code: 03-02

124. **Answer: b. Scheduled after an employment offer has been extended.** The Americans with Disabilities Act prohibits medical examinations before the extension of an employment offer. Results of a medical examination can then be used in making reasonable accommodations. Code: 02-01

125. **Answer: b. Referring a qualified personal friend's resume for an open position in another department.** Although all the options are potential ethical dilemmas for the HR manager, referring the resume of a qualified friend to an open position in another department is the least problematic. As long as the HR manager does not advocate for the selection of the friend, no ethics violation would occur. To deny the referral based on friendship would deny a qualified candidate equal opportunity. Skewing salary survey data for self-betterment is clearly an ethics violation. Likewise, breaches of confidentiality are ethics violations. Code: 01-10

SECTION V:

FREQUENTLY ASKED QUESTIONS

The following questions are those most frequently asked about the HR Certification Institute and its certification program. The questions and answers are grouped into the following areas:

- Exam application.
- Exam preparation.
- HR body of knowledge.
- The certification exams.
- Exam administration.
- Recertification.

EXAM APPLICATION

Q. Why would my application be returned or deemed ineligible?

A. The most common reasons that applications are returned are:

- Not including payment with the application.
- Sending a personal check rather than credit card payment (Visa, MasterCard or American Express only), money order, cashier's check or organizational check.
- Not including supporting documentation, if needed.
- Submitting a faxed or photocopied application.

The most common reasons for deeming an application ineligible are:

- Receiving the application after the late registration postmark date.
- Not having the required professional (exempt-level) HR work experience and/or education.

Q. Are exam fees reduced for SHRM members?

A. Yes. The HR Certification Institute is a separate organization from SHRM. However, SHRM founded the HR Certification Institute and financially supported it for many years. Today, the Institute is self-supporting. The reduced exam fee for SHRM members is a professional courtesy to SHRM in appreciation for those early years of support.

Q. Why does the HR Certification Institute require professional (exempt-level) HR work experience to be eligible to take the exam?

A. The HR Certification Institute grants professional certification in the human resource management field. Certification is not granted for paraprofessional or other nonexempt experience. Because these are practice-based exams, it is important that candidates have actual work experience in the areas being tested. Candidates must have an executive, administrative or professional exemption under the Fair Labor Standards Act to be eligible to take the PHR, SPHR or GPHR exam.

Q. Because the body of knowledge is the same for the PHR and SPHR exams, how do I determine which exam to take?

A. If you have at least two to four years of professional (exempt-level) HR work experience in combination with the appropriate educational background, you should consider taking the PHR exam. If you have a broad range of HR experience/education and six to eight years of experience, it might be appropriate to take the SPHR exam. The most important thing is to take the exam that best demonstrates your mastery of the PHR and SPHR Body of Knowledge.

EXAM PREPARATION

Q. What is the best way to prepare?

A. There is no single best way to prepare. A lot depends on your education and background in human resources, your learning style and your lifestyle. Select a preparation method that best matches each of these areas. It might be a highly flexible approach such as individual self-study, or a moderately structured approach such as a preparation course or the SHRM Learning System. In any case, remember that the exam tests your mastery of the U.S. body of knowledge and it is impossible to teach to the test. Candidates must master the HR Certification Institute's test specifications and be able to apply those specifications.

Q. Does the HR Certification Institute recommend learning resources?

A. No, we do not endorse any one learning resource as being qualitatively better than another and generally recommend that candidates use multiple reference materials when studying for the exams. At the same time, those resources based upon the PHR/SPHR test specifications may better prepare candidates for the tests.

Q. How do I know if I am ready to take the exam?

A. Review the PHR/SPHR test specifications. If you can honestly say that you are comfortable with each of the responsibilities and knowledge areas in the outline, you are probably a good candidate to take the exam. Consider taking a self-assessment exam to see how you perform.

PHR AND SPHR BODY OF KNOWLEDGE

Q. Why are the PHR/SPHR test specifications so important?

A. Test specifications are the blueprint for the HR Certification Institute's exams. The weightings on the specifications correspond to the weightings on the exam. Candidates will only be tested on subject matter included in the test specifications.

Q. How often does the HR Certification Institute revise its test specifications?

A. The PHR and SPHR Body of Knowledge undergoes major revision approximately every five years. Minor revisions may occur annually as a result of expert or literature reviews and to reflect changes in HR laws.

THE CERTIFICATION EXAMS

Q. Where do the exam questions come from?

A. Test questions, or items, are written by certified HR professionals, not by academics or professional test developers. Because the questions are developed by certified HR professionals, they tend to be very practical and applied. Exam scores correlate with years of experience and education.

Q. How reliable are the exams?

A. Very reliable. If you do not pass an exam and decide to re-take it without extensive preparation or additional experience, your results will be similar to the first time you took the exam.

Q. Are the HR Certification Institute's exams validated?

A. Yes, our exams are content validated. The blueprints for PHR and SPHR exams come from the PHR/SPHR test specifications. Those specifications are the result of the HR Certification Institute's practice analysis process—a job analysis of sorts for the entire HR field. Only questions that correspond to the test specifications are used on the exams. Contributing to this content-validation model is the fact that the HR Certification Institute uses only certified HR professionals to write items, review them, evaluate test forms and analyze the performance of exams. PHR/SPHR test specifications conform to the highest standards in the certification testing field.

Q. What is the best predictor of success on the exam?

A. HR education and professional (exempt-level) work experience are the best predictors of success on the HR Certification Institute's exams.

Q. What is the difference between a raw score and a scaled score?

A. A raw score is the actual number of items answered correctly on the exam. A scaled score is placed on a uniform scale and reflects differences in difficulty levels of different forms of the same exam. A scaled score ensures that every examinee, no matter when he or she took the exam, achieves the same uniform standard. A passing score on an HR Certification Institute exam is a scaled score of 500. This process ensures consistency and fairness among exam forms.

Q. Are certain functional areas of the exam more difficult than others?

A. The answer is based on the education and experience candidates bring to the exam. For instance, candidates who have never worked in a unionized environment could find items on employee and labor relations more difficult than would those candidates with experience in labor relations. It is really an individual matter. Each of the exam's functional areas includes questions with a fairly broad range of difficulty levels.

Q. Why are PHR and SPHR exams weighted differently?

A. PHR and SPHR exams differ in terms of focus and the cognitive level of questions. PHR exam questions tend to be at the operational/technical level, and the SPHR questions tend to be at the strategic and/or policy level. Therefore, a major emphasis on the SPHR exam is in business management and strategy.

Q. Are questions on the PHR exam different from those on the SPHR exam?

A. Yes, PHR questions tend to be technical and operational. They involve the cognitive abilities of recall and comprehension. SPHR questions tend to be more policy-oriented and strategic. They test the ability to analyze and synthesize, often using scenario questions.

Q. What is a scenario question?

A. A scenario question includes a paragraph (called an information set) that provides basic information about a given situation. It is followed by a series of four-answer multiple-choice items. Scenario questions are ideal for the SPHR exam because they require candidates to integrate information from more than one functional area of the test specifications to arrive at a correct answer. Scenario items reflect situations commonly encountered by senior-level HR practitioners.

Q. Do I have to memorize the year a law was passed?

A. The exams do not test trivia! It is not important to know what year (1935) the Wagner Act passed, but candidates should know how to identify an unfair labor practice. Remember, exam questions are very practical and applied.

Q. If I don't know the answer to a question, should I leave it blank?

A. No. Scoring is based on the number of correct answers. A guess is far better than leaving a question blank.

EXAM ADMINISTRATION

Q. I have a disability. Can I be accommodated at the exam site?

A. The HR Certification Institute complies with the Americans with Disabilities Act as amended, covering facilities and administration. Candidates with special accommodations should submit a request with supporting documentation at the time of application. Please see the HR Certification Institute's Certification Handbook for more information about these procedures. Handbooks can be viewed or downloaded online at www.hrci.org.

Q. Do I need a calculator to take the exam?

A. No. Most exam questions are designed to be answered without a calculator. One will be available on the desktop of your computer at the testing center, just in case.

Q. What should I do if I fail?

A. Start by reviewing your detailed score report, which will be sent to you in the mail a few weeks after you have taken the exam. All score reports show the raw scores (number correct) for each of the functional areas. This should help you identify areas that need improvement when considering additional preparation. You must wait until the next exam period to re-take the exam, and you must re-apply and pay the required fees.

Q. Can I review my test results or get a list of the questions I missed?

A. Because of test security, test results and question/answer documents are not available for review. If you have questions about your exam, you may contact the HR Certification Institute at (866) 898-4724.

RECERTIFICATION

Q. How do I recertify?

A. Recertification is required every three years by the expiration date of the current certification cycle. Recertification can be achieved by successfully re-testing or by documenting 60 hours of continuing education activities that update HR knowledge and/or experience.

Q. What education and experience counts toward the 60 recertification credit hours needed to recertify?

A. Activities in the following categories can count toward recertification:

- Continuing education.

- Research and/or publishing.

- Instruction/teaching.

- On-the-job experience.

- HR leadership.

- Professional membership.

Q. How was the three-year time frame determined for recertification?

A. The determination was made by the HR Certification Institute's board in recognition of the amount and speed of change occurring in the HR field.

Please visit www.hrci.org for more information about the recertification process, a recertification application form and access to your online recertification file (once you have been certified).